FIVE KEYS TO

Productivity and Profits

FIVE KEYS TO

Productivity and Profits

A. GORDON BRADT

Parker Publishing Company, Inc.

West Nyack, New York

Library of Congress Cataloging in Publication Data

Bradt, Acken Gordon.
  Five keys to productivity and profits.

  1. Success. 2. Management. I. Title.
HF5386.B74   658   72-10159
ISBN 0-13-321562-8

Printed in the United States of America

To my wife, Aliff, with appreciation for her invaluable contributions in reviewing the manuscript and her constant help in completing this work.

HOW THIS BOOK WILL
WORK FOR YOU

This book will help you
—make your people outstanding performers
—raise department productivity to record highs
—cut your turnover in half
—stop costs from eating into profits
—create new profits through many cost savings
—insure high quality for your products and services
—increase your sales sharply
—multiply your own productive talents
—realize rich rewards in promotion, income and career growth.
You hold in this book five sure keys to these results and to many more.

Your success as a winning manager—and you may be that now—centers completely on your ability to lift your department to high standards of productivity and profit. The greatest single force for profit are people who go all-out in the work they do, and the greatest single desire of people is to make their work count to the fullest for them. Managers who bring together this No. 1 force and this No. 1 desire to achieve high performance results are the top generators of profits for their organizations. Business can never get enough of this kind of manager. He moves far and fast in any field.

Productivity is widely recognized as your No. 1 weapon to slash rising costs, up the quality and sale of your products and services at competitive prices, generate new earning power and promotion opportunities for you and the people reporting to you. Increasing productivity is the one force that will do the job for you. The reverse spells spiralling expenses that shrink profits and sales, slam shut your doors to advancement growth. Peak production is your master stroke to lick your worst problems. How do you get peak production?

There are two major costs which can cut deep into your profits: payroll and materials. Economic forces block you from doing much about the second. You can do a lot about the high cost of people. People become your finest investment or your biggest expense. People make profits or eat into them. It all depends on what you do to *tap the power of talent where you are.*

Study after study shows that most people use but a small fraction of their abilities. Each manager's payroll dollars are working only part time unless something very specific is done about it. The greatest single opportunity for profit and growth for every manager is to tap the deep reservoir of productive capacity in each person. How do you do this? Here in one sure, all-ready-to-apply, step-by-step package—this book—you hold *five powerful keys* to unlock these talents, lift your department as its manager or supervisor to new highs in people performance. You see this being done and just how they do it in over 200 situations drawn from top operating departments in many fields. You see people become high producers by applying their maximum abilities together with the best technological skills.

Every quick-reading chapter of this book gives you the master tools and specific ways to develop to the fullest the resources of each member of your department, senior and junior. Each page contains up-to-the-minute techniques to bring you top production. Here are a few examples:

  —What makes it exciting for a person to perform at top speed, see pages 23–31.
  —The supervisor is the key to slashing turnover costs, see pages 53 and 55.
  —Removing blocks to high output, see page 58.
  —Where productivity and profits get away, see page 59.
  —Five moves to high productivity make the job fun, see page 62.
  —Tap a whole new world of customers, see pages 75–80.
  —The secret to effective communications, see page 98.

—Three profit moves to make *now,* see page 107.

—How to solve operating, management, or customer service problems quickly, see page 127.

—Turn twenty-six "people problems" into "people profits," see pages 127–133.

—What the individual on the job really wants to know to produce, see page 138.

—How to answer ten questions which concern people most, see pages 140–141.

—Money does talk! See pages 154–155.

—Pay plans take top priority, see page 156.

—Raise productivity? Do away with dead-end jobs, see page 168.

—Earnings tripled through profit sharing, see page 173.

—Six qualities *make* a leader, and build people fast, see pages 197–215.

—How you can profit most where you are, see page 211.

Your Finest Opportunity Is Ahead

Demands for you who are top producers can come from all sides because of unprecedented needs. Projections show that within ten years, one-half of the executives in business will have successors in their places. On top of that, expansion will bring a fifty percent increase in management openings over and above these man-for-man replacements. Sixty to eighty thousand new key spots must be filled at a time when the number of people available for management jobs will shrink by one million in the decade ahead.

Your opportunity to move far by increasing productivity is in every growing company, but greatest in the service field. Twice as many people will be needed here as in all other industries. The main thrust of the U.S. economy has shifted from producing goods to performing services. This is where two-thirds of the employees of this country now are. Within ten years the number of U.S. families will grow by more than fifteen million, generating multiple demands for a wide range of services and products. On top of these needs will be calls from millions of established families moving into higher earnings. Are you ready to meet these demands and opportunities where you are? You will be when you take hold of and apply *now* the Five Keys to Productivity and Profits.

Included in each key's many tools are proven, result-producing personnel development programs all ready for you to make your own. You are shown exactly how to use them to get the maximum returns you want. Start putting each one to work for you by turning first to Key One.

———*A. Gordon Bradt*

CONTENTS

MASTER TOOLS

EXHIBITS

KEY ONE

Giant Motivators to Peak Performance

"He's got one speed—all-out!" said an All American football coach of his varsity guard who shot from mediocrity to a standout performer in one short season. A lightweight among today's giants, he has a small face and stubby fingers, and every other coach knows that offensive guards must have large faces and mighty hands to match. How does he do it?

"Personal pride, and always thinking I'm better than the other guy until he knocks me on my butt."

"Knocking him on his butt *once* doesn't do it," says his coach.

Realizing that he was being counted on to open holes where there were none, he went all-out on every play. Game-breaking touchdowns came through his position. He knew only *one speed*.

Managers, supervisors, and presidents across the U.S. face a crucial need for *one-speed performance* in many quarters to raise productivity far above present levels. No other force affects profits half as much. How do you accomplish it? Every page of this book tells how.

To start, go with me inside a company that is an established aggressive leader. Already out in front in its earnings and growth, it is alive to the demand for getting people to be not just good performers, but outstanding performers. Watch this company's key managers shoot ideas across a table.

Their interlocutor, Jim Barlow, executive vice president, outlines their target. "We see the impact on profits and costs when our people brought their performance up eleven percent. But we know there are individuals in business after business—they are on our payroll—who are using but a small fraction of their capacity to produce. Studies show that a typical person uses less than ten percent of his or her productive abilities. Think what it means then to each person and his company to triple his output by tapping into this ninety percent of his unused power. How do we do it?''

Ideas explode from this group.

"How do you get the best out of a man? It depends a lot on the environment he is in. Someone says to me, 'Look at George Drake, don't you think he's a great guy?' No, I don't think he's such a great guy. Sure, he's a good performer, but not a great performer. Why? The environment in which the man is placed governs his ability to produce at his best. That environment may be a manager who either believes in him or doesn't believe in him. How he relates to his environment is all-important."

"I've got a guy who only gives me a super job when I chew him out good. He likes it and he performs. I chew out another guy and he crumbles under it. How he relates to the environment of his boss and how that boss relates to him can make all the difference."

"I find most individuals need to be 'hungry,' low or middle class and even crude when compared to the smooth, well-heeled guys in the upper crust."

"How do you define hunger?"

"Hunger can be expressed in physical things, but often more in desperately wanting recognition, companionship, love, or craving to be needed."

"It can be hunger to get even with a world that gave him a raw deal at some time."

"Hunger is important in a group, because only a hungry man can go through what we've been through."

"Hungry or not, to me it all starts with the manager. There has to be something in that manager which says that you will give more for him than for another."

"He's a manager who puts the individual in a work situation that he enjoys."

"He sets an example that he can follow."

"He knows how to differentiate between a passable and a superior performance."

"The individual must above all believe that his personal interest will be protected by his manager."

"Some managers operate on the belief that the motivator which works best to get the most out of people is *fear.*"

"Fear of what?"

"Fear of failure. Most men will go all-out on their job for fear of having to tell their wife. 'How do I explain it to her?' Or fear of what family and friends will think."

"Is what's in it for me, *in money,* the big incentive?"

"That is only part of it. The one thing that pulls him to the ultimate in performance is his achieving the ultimate regardless of the money involved."

"What part does belief in himself, that 'I can do it' play?"

"With some individuals it means everything."

"To go all-out, a person has to believe in himself every inch of the way."

"But you've got to give him that belief by believing in him yourself and showing him that you believe in him. If you don't, he may never make it."

"I find self-satisfaction out of accomplishing a job at peak performance motivates many people."

"Yes, but it takes more. Keep giving him a part of the action. 'Let me do it myself' is vital to him. He can feel himself taking the reins."

"Make sure he sees that his part is essential to getting a top job done."

"Watch letting a person think you're working psychology on him. He reads you fast."

"How honest is your relationship with him? Let down here at any time and you're through."

"What motivates us to do our best is often a sense of urgency, when you feel that 'this has to be done.' "

"The individual must see that success is rewarded across the board. Playing favorites will kill you."

"To get people to go all-out, be flexible at every turn. The challenge for a manager is his ability to deal with this group, and this group, and this group. You have to be able to shift fast, change your approach, your style."

"To get people to give that top extra, you need to set the pace."

"Be sure they know what is expected of them."

"Set high performance standards, then reward the individuals who reach them."

"How?"

"Through recognition, promotion, advancement, money comes with it."

"And if he doesn't reach the high standard?"

"Help him correct his weak points, build on his strong ones, so he does reach it, so you *can* reward him."

"He's got to know you care about him, honestly care."

"Keep before him the *fun* factor, a tremendous motivator. The job becomes fun for him the moment he changes from average to a super-performer."

"A manager who gets top performance understands what that person wants for himself."

"The spur for me to go all-out is that by doing so I have some influence on my own destiny, get control over my own future. That's what I want."

"Help him know he is important to the success of the business. This can trigger him to make his finest contribution."

"To give your best you've got to *know your business,* and this doesn't just happen. It means equipping each person with specific company-wide know-why, know-how education and training (Key Two). This unlocks his ninety percent unused ability fast, for him and his employer."

"To me the prime motivator is this: You can get performance as such out of any number of people, but it takes a *Crusade Environment—the Dominant Idea—*to inspire his best."

"The Dominant Idea? That's central. That's how this business started. It is the *thrust* that keeps moving it ahead . . ."

Above are thirty result-producing ideas to get people to perform at top speed. They come out of a live-action managerial huddle you have just been a part of in one of the country's most successful companies.

Take these ideas and make them yours. Begin capitalizing on them now. They lead right into your use of one of the top motivators to high production. Chapter 1 has the story.

1

Unleash the Dominant Idea

Would you make it exciting for a person to perform at top speed? Give him the Dominant Idea!

Ideas dominate—as a man thinks, so is he. Ideas are to the mind what nourishment is to the body. Ideas are nourishing to both mind and body if they are true ideas.

No person rises higher than his ideas or ideals. The dominant idea shapes the success of every individual as it does his company. Both rise or fall on that *idea*.

"There are three things I want out of my job," said a young manager in a dynamic Chicago company.

"1. Control over my future

  2. Opportunity to go as far as my ability will take me, to bring out my best

  3. Fun and satisfaction in knowing what I do counts to the full."

Each of these goals contains a dominant idea that triggers high output for more than 22,000 managers and their people in companies across the U.S. and abroad. In face-to-face experience with these managers, with individuals on jobs, senior and junior, this message comes through from all sides:

> Managers need to make clear that each person's job offers him far more than pay and pay increases, far more than profit

sharing, pension, insurance, hospitalization, and incentive programs, more than the whole package of benefits currently available.

Over and above these things a company must assure the
individual, and he must earn this assurance by performance, that
he has control over his own future, that he is vitally important
to the products and services he, by his own efforts, helps to make
possible.

Show him that he is essential to meeting the needs and satisfac-
tions of customers.

Let him understand that he has only begun to tap the talents
within him, to move as far as his abilities will take him.

To gain these goals, find the dominant idea in your job and your
business.

What is the dominant idea? It is the all-consuming purpose which
inspires a company and its members to produce superior products
or services at the lowest practical cost to meet the growing needs
of more and more people with increasing profit to the company and
to each person who makes it all possible. This dominant idea brings
a business into being, makes it, builds it, opens wide its future and
the future of each one contributing to it.

Every growing company has this dominant idea. It is its life line
to success at every point.

"What is the dominant idea that makes and builds a bank?" a
customer asked his banker.

He got this answer: "It is that a bank can do more things for
more people in more ways than any other business or profession anywhere. Why? Because *money is life,* a product of the ideas and energies of people in every business. Into the banks of this nation and the
world goes this lifeblood of industry all the way from the soil clear
through to the consumer."

But you may say quickly: "Wait a minute! With the products and
services of our business and what we can do for people, our dominant idea is greater than that."

Exactly. If your business is successful and growing, you can be
sure it holds a dominant idea for you that can be a master booster
for productivity and profits for you and your company.

How do you uncover this dominant idea? There are three sure ways.

One: Find the dominant idea in the romance of your business.

That romance is rooted in the story that gave birth to your company. It is the story of what you make possible for people through your products and services. Every business has that romance. Without it your company would shrivel and die.

Capture that idea *now* and make sure you get it into the consciousness of each person around you. Visualize what the dominant idea means to him, his job, his future.

This idea may be born on a tennis court. It was for Foster G. McGaw, founder of American Hospital Supply Corporation. During a match with his future partner came an idea to form his own firm to sell surgical instruments to hospitals. Doctors at that time were buying their own instruments even for use in hospitals. McGaw felt that the hospitals (which then purchased mainly linen and food) were the real market place for medical supplies.

The new company they formed was so poor he and his partner insisted that the lawyer who helped them organize take a share of stock instead of the hundred dollar fee he wanted. Later when the lawyer died, that single share had split and multiplied into more than 20,000 shares with a value of nearly $700,000.

McGaw Rode in the Caboose

Charged with his dominant idea, McGaw started making regular rounds to hospital customers even though it sometimes meant riding freight train cabooses.

"I felt we had to take our business to the hospitals, not ask them to come to us," said McGaw.

Starting in Iowa, he called on every one of his hospital customers once a month, much to their amazement.

How the Idea Spread

Beginning as a midwestern distribution operation, the firm branched into the manufacturing field. Out of McGaw's dominant idea grew more than forty manufacturing locations, producing everything from artificial heart valves and organ preservation systems to disposable syringes and pharmaceuticals; and ninety distribution centers, reaching 120 countries with their products.

The dominant idea to meet world-wide health needs of people in unique ways is projected into the thinking and performance of some 14,000 of the firm's employees, including microbiologists, engineers, salesmen, physicists, doctors and dieticians. How was this done? By person-to-person relationships and confidence built by each manager and supervisor with the individual on the job.

How do you build this confidence? In a highly structured corporate society, McGaw kept telling his managers: "Be sure the line of communications from you to the last in line *is an open one*, so that anyone from top to bottom feels free to approach you about any problem, personal or business."

The Dominant Idea Is in Every Job

To generate all-out individual performance, dominant ideas do not need to be as dramatic as those coming out of the McGaw story. Many a dominant idea, insignificant at the start, gets major results. The key is in the next step.

Two: Realize that without the dominant idea what we do has no meaning. We just go through motions.

Unless we get hold of the *idea* that makes our job and our future, we are "spinning our wheels," putting on our clothes each morning, for what? Millions around us do that.

The other day a small boy said to his mother, "Mom, you say we are made out of dust and when we die we go back to dust?"

"Yes, my son, but why do you ask?"

"Well," replied the little fellow, "I just looked under my bed, and somebody is either coming or going."

On all sides you see that happening in business after business, people coming and going on jobs, without realizing what they are doing, why they are doing it, or where they are headed.

These lines depict what is happening *now* to many individuals on myriads of jobs.

LIFE

The ways of Providence are inscrutable,
And past all finding out.
The laws of living are immutable,
They are beyond a doubt.
And man he is a feeble thing,
A poor fate-tortured sinner,
A slave unto his breakfast,
His luncheon and his dinner.

One-third of time he spends in bed,
One-eighth he spends in eating,
One-third in working that he may
These things keep on repeating.
He shaves himself and combs his hair
And bathes and trims his nails.
Puts on his clothes and takes them off
But naught he does avail.
He wakes to sleep and sleeps to wake
And eats that his digestion
May prompt him soon to eat again,
But why, that is the question.

The hair and whiskers he cuts off
Grow out to need more cutting.
His eyes are scarcely opened
When the time comes for their shutting.
In those odd hours he spends
From working, eating, sleeping,
He does a little hoping, vain
And loving, laughing, weeping.
He calls this futile program "Life"
But knows that he is lying.
For truth points out that living
Is but the mere process of dying.

Anonymous

"Why am I here?"
"What is life all about?"
There are people all around you in job after job, in company after

company, living like the man in this poem. They are squirrels in a cage going around and around, without meaning, without purpose, without objective.

Dwight L. Moody, in early transportation days, was seated with a friend in a railroad car, wondering why the car did not move. He hailed a passing trainman and asked, "What's the matter with this car?"

The trainman replied, "Nothing the matter with it, Mister, nothing at all. The only trouble is it isn't hitched to anything that's going anywhere."

Motivation, inspiration, the dominant idea! That's what discovered America. It is what George Washington called "that little spark of celestial fire."

Thomas A. Edison, when asked what he considered his greatest invention, replied without hesitation, "the incandescent lamp," because Edison knew that while he slept his marvelous invention was being used in the world's hospitals twenty-four hours a day in the operating rooms saving human life.

Your job as a leader, as a manager, supervisor, or president, is to "turn on the lights," give meaning and purpose to the productive efforts of each member on your team, show what each one accomplishes for customers and their own advancement. When you unleash the dominant idea in an individual, you trigger untapped productive talents he never knew he had because the dominant idea was never his until you gave it to him.

Morton Kort, head of a fast-growing merchandising company, visualized his organization's dominant idea in this way: "Everything we do must be directed to providing desired and appreciated consumer services or we lose our reason for being."

The greatest thrust of the dominant idea on individual performance often comes with the next step.

Three: Develop the idea with each person that he or she has a contribution to make which no one else can make.

"You are you. Each person is different from every other person anywhere. You have your own individual contribution to make on your job to both your own and the company's profit." One of the best ways to find this contribution for you and for those reporting to you, is to get hold of the dominant idea *in your job*.

This is exactly what Ron Bates did. Ron was an accountant in the treasurer's office of the Browning Company, making and selling a diversified line of sporting goods and athletic equipment. Ron dealt with figures all day long. At times it seemed that he was in a terribly dull business. Then something happened. The treasurer invited him to lunch to talk about the department's work. During the conversation he stressed the importance of accounting procedures and the interpretation of figures as the backbone of the company.

> "You and I know, Ron, that these money figures also represent what money does translated into skiing, bowling, golf, fishing, football, baseball, basketball and the equipment that goes with such sports and which brings enjoyment to growing multitudes of individuals and families.
>
> "What we do with figures is also translated into savings in taxes, one of the high-cost fields where accounting processes make a major impact. Figures and what we do with them make possible incentive programs and profit-sharing plans which lead to increased individual production on the part of many people in this company and the resulting rewards they receive.
>
> "Working with figures helps bring about new financing and new sources of funds to expand the company's activities.
>
> "When any of us uncovers ways to accomplish these goals, we make a direct contribution to company profits and to the value of our jobs. . . ."

Visiting with the treasurer started Ron Bates thinking of a dominant idea tailor-made for him. With a background of law, he had been interested in this field of taxes although it was not a part of his current work. He decided to begin an intensive study of corporate taxation on his own. Three weeks later the treasurer asked Ron to make a special tax study for the company. It proved to be so productive in savings that it brought him the position of treasurer, tripling his salary when his boss was suddenly made president.

Find the Dominant Idea Where You Are

You and each person around you have your own experience and special talents no one else possesses. Find your own dominant idea and capitalize on it.

Bob Turney, 29, was teaching ecology at a state university, following employment with a large manufacturing firm in Ohio. He was determined to put his academic, specialized knowledge to work in a practical way. He resigned his professorship, took a purchasing job with a medium-sized manufacturer of pumps and other equipment to combat water pollution.

Purchasing was the last thing Bob wanted to do, but it was the only opening the company had. He made the combination of his new job with his pollution control studies *his dominant idea*. In two years he cut purchasing costs in half with his management techniques, gave the sales force new competitive selling points on what their pumps and auxiliary products can do. Now he not only heads purchasing, but is associate director of sales with a future ahead that shows no limits.

The Dominant Idea Opens Two Doors

Vincent Toder, 27, employed as sales correspondent with Power Tools Corporation, is a student in our university management courses.

"A very fine promotion has just come my way," he said, "and it is due to making my dominant idea the study of personnel management and the development of people."

This company, growing fast both nationally and internationally, has been so chained down with other functions that its attention to these two major areas became tragically deficient. Turnover of people had more than doubled.

"They told me," he said, "to set up a pilot education and training program (Key Two) in my department, preparatory to my helping to initiate it company wide. This is the first part of a double-header assignment. My boss asked me to move fast in recommending an overall personnel management and development program geared to each individual, senior and junior (Key Four in chapter 11). It is all hit and miss now. The road ahead is what I make it."

When the Dominant Idea Gets Hold of You

We see how productivity shoots up when we get hold of the dominant idea. But the greatest result can take place when this order is reversed and the dominant idea gets hold of *you*. When this happens it controls everything you do. Because of it you put out fresh energy.

It got a king-sized grip on Carl Doran, one of our top students. Carl's ship was shot out from under him in World War II. He spent three years and seven months in Iwo Jima as a Japanese prisoner of war. Over half the men captured with him died in the prison camp. Carl's dominant idea got him out of there after twice being at death's edge. He went with a paper company and, while supporting a family, he took sixty-three hours of credit in university night courses to gain his B.S. degree. Continuing to hold down a full-time job, he moved fast. Today he is general manager of his company, with his throttle of opportunity wide open.

"The dominant idea took hold of me in that prison camp and wouldn't let go," laughed Carl. "From then on it's been my life saver."

The experiences cited in this chapter are drawn from hundreds that are taking place each day. They are typical of the multiple opportunities developing for many managers and individuals in job after job when their dominant idea takes hold of them.

Look at your own situation right now. Where is the dominant idea in that situation? One very effective way to uncover it and put it to work for you is in meeting the tremendous desires of people reporting to you. Turn to the chapter ahead.

2

Trigger Six
Tremendous Desires

In face-to-face studies with thirty leading companies in ten countries we asked two questions:

1. "What factor contributes most to your growth?" Their answers gave this clear message: "Our greatest factor is our competitive advantage *won* by the performance of our people."
2. "How do you get your people to produce at their best?" "By making every effort to meet six basic individual desires," was the reply given on all sides.

These findings are backed by the experiences of companies across America of every size and in many fields. These desires when met move people to go all-out in their work. They become giant motivators in your hands to unlock productive talents that have been there right along waiting for you to tap them. These desires are listed below.

I. *Recognition* of each person as an individual making his own contribution

Today this craving for recognition supplants opportunity as the No. 1 desire, for with recognition comes opportunity.

"Individual recognition is more important than pay in Venezuela," said the young manager of a Caracas oil company. "Our people have a strong sense of pride in what they themselves accomplish and if s is not recognized they will leave you, even if you pay them more. Recognition is an overriding factor throughout Latin America.

"I have this 'recognition check list' that helps me do something about it each day with people reporting to me:

- Make yourself easily accessible to talk to your people about problems in selling prospects or in organizing their work.
- Encourage people to work *with* you, not for you.
- Tell them in advance about changes that affect them.
- Give credit when due. Be quick to compliment.
- Make sure each person knows what is expected and how he is doing.
- Let each person know he is solidly on your team and that you will back him up when he needs it.

"Does it pay off? Our production is up forty percent."

Lifting the Individual Out of the Crowd

"*Recognition* is the top morale booster," said Ed Brodie, supervisor with Balmer Utilities Company. "We have many programs to do this. At the top in effectiveness is taking the word 'employees' and 'officers' out of our vocabulary in all our communications spoken and written. In writing we address them together as 'members' of our company."

"Employees? What's wrong with that word?" he was asked.

"It blots out identity with a caste label. We've become a nation of employees. Each person working with me is an individual person, making his or her own contribution to our products and services for our customers."

"One of the best ways to show individual recognition and to trigger performance," said Marvin Kass, manager at Manton Automotive Company, "is to promote people every chance you have, whether in your department or out of it. I've asked our personnel director to let me know of every opening that develops to see if I have a recommendation to make."

Multiply Your Individual Talents

A leading photographic studio firm has a unique way of recognizing the individual and his own special talents. One of the senior photographers heads a class in color photography for all members of the organization. Another is teaching a full class in taking portrait pictures. Both talents are being multiplied in each of their studios. Two major results: (1) many new customers are being won by the special high quality of the studios' products; (2) two senior photographers-turned-instructors have new careers with new incomes, while being recognized for contributions to their firm no one else has made.

Now link recognition with the second desire and you have twin engines of productivity that have no limits.

II. *Opportunity* for full use of one's talents

"Opportunity means everything to me," said a national representative of a U.S. oil company in Brazil. "I am a prime illustration of an individual who would instantly trade money and my many benefits of living here for opportunity at our headquarters in the States. Here I have superb office facilities, with secretary and office assistants, my own car furnished by my company, all club memberships, social and business prestige, tuition for our son in private school paid by the company, extra compensation for living abroad, thirty-four days vacation each year, three months leave every three years, we own a condominium house in a beautiful setting in the hills, golf course membership, being my own boss, perfect weather and climate, and clear sea air.

"I would quickly sacrifice all of this to move to Chicago's zero weather to have the opportunity of being an important individual on the team, a chance to use my full talents, to be in on decisions, to show what I can do."

A few months later this young Brazilian was given his headquarters opportunity and is now in the throes of battling for position on a fast track. But he was never happier.

Ways to capitalize on this powerful desire are in companies of all sizes.

"We are taking a new look at every job to see if it shows daylight ahead," said Roy Panter, department supervisor with Pyton Regulator Company. "If it doesn't, we are restructuring or mechanizing it where practical. This move is made not just because people want opportunity in the work they do. We find that by studying the job's content we can often make its operation more efficient. With individual opportunity comes both increased performance and substantial cost savings."

The myth that hosts of people are content to sit on dead-end jobs because they are easy to do, with no worries and little responsibility while they draw their breath and their salary, is fast exploding with the onrush of education and the realization that more pay goes hand in hand with more responsibility. Even young women, waiting to marry or now married and filling jobs until they have babies, today go after better-paying opportunities to offset their shrinking dollars.

Your Ceiling Is What You Make It

The desire of people in every business for opportunity to make the most of their talents has blown to bits a doctrine preached by some academic psychologists and personnel practitioners: "Most people reach a limit of where they can go. They become boxed in, bumping their heads against their ceiling. They should be happy with their lot, content to cough along on their one cylinder."

These little minds try to play God every day, to put on the cat and mouse act with the most valuable asset in their companies. How long? Until they're found out. And this happens in a hurry in companies who go only with "profit makers" not "profit killers."

Their shallow thinking embraced one or both of these philosophies:

1. The abilities of most "employees" are quite low. To try to rise above their incompetence results in great unhappiness and job disaster. So avoid frustration by never reaching your level of incompetence, your final placement.
2. Work expands to fill the time available. In any organization the number of subordinates multiplies at a predetermined annual rate regardless of the amount of work that the staff actually turns out.

Both approaches give the human race a low-ability ceiling. Enlightened managers across the world operate on a totally different principle: "We have only begun to tap the possibilities in the individual, and he is happiest when his talents are fully used. Management's job in every department is to equip each one to make the most of his opportunities. The rich rewards that follow are not just in money, but in realizing goals achieved by abilities he never knew he had."

How do you help him do this? One of the surest ways is to meet a deep universal desire of each person. What is it?

III. *Seeing his place on the team.* **He knows he fills a vital spot—management is counting on him.**

Show him what his specific performance means to the success of your department, your products and services, to satisfied customers, to profits, and to his own future. Do this by talking with him individually on schedule. People this minute are working in companies with ten, fifty, a hundred others around them, yet feeling like they are on a desert island, lost in the organization.

"Nobody in management ever actually talks with me," said George Konder, who does his work efficiently, quietly. "They take me for granted. The other day a desk was moved out of here. What happened to that guy? I hear they're cutting down on personnel. Am I next? Where is my company headed? What do profits look like? What's cooking? Where am I headed?"

Too often, unless we are careful, people go along on their jobs month after month without their boss ever sitting down with them individually on his own initiative to talk *with* them about questions or mutual problems, about their jobs, their place on the team.

Here is a bank teller, Jim White, who has just waited on a customer and is worried because he has an uneasy feeling that he had not handled the customer's transaction the right way. Considerable money was involved, so he looks over at his boss's desk to see if he is available to talk with him about it. But the boss is on the telephone, or talking with another customer, or is in a meeting away from his desk. In frustration he says to himself: "Every time I want to see that guy he's busy. Well, I'm busy too. My time is worth something. So I'll just skip it."

The next day his boss passes him on the banking floor without even saying "good morning" to him. It was an unconscious omission. He was thinking about something else. But Jim puts the two unconnected incidents together and thinks, "I must be really in the doghouse now. He didn't even say 'good morning' to me." And so molehills grow into mountains, all because he did not have a chance to talk over his question with the one to whom he reports.

An "Open Door Policy" Is Not Enough

Somebody says, "Oh, I have the open door policy. My door is always open. Come in any time."

Do they come in? Most people are timid. Even a fellow officer hesitates to barge up to his boss and open up on a question or problem that is bothering him no end. So he just skips it and as time goes by it becomes magnified beyond all proportions. Such discussions in which the boss *makes* the opportunity by initiating the conversation himself can lift the morale of the whole organization, whether there are a few people or hundreds.

It did more than that for the bank where Jim White works. Jim's experience with his manager started a program of scheduled individual interviews throughout the bank that raised people productivity more than fourteen percent, helped send earnings to new highs. Jim himself saw in this bank-wide communications program a chance to work for a senior spot in the organization, and is now the bank's chief operating officer.

Seeing his place on the team leads to a fourth desire loaded with incentives to all-out effort.

IV. *Enjoyment* of his work, and his business in a congenial environment without *undue* pressures

If we are not getting any fun out of our job, whatever our responsibility, do something about it. Life is too short to spend our waking hours on work we don't relish. This does not mean a job free from pressures. There are pressures on any job worth doing. We live in a competitive world. All life is competitive. We must keep fighting to maintain our health. No matter how healthy we feel, let down our guard physically or mentally and disaster can hit.

Normal pressures in any job are par for the course. It's the abnormal, undue pressures that take the fun out of what you're doing, cuts to the quick your productive efforts and those of people reporting to you who are in similar straits. But *undue* pressures in one job may be entirely normal in another's business.

People in a bank, big or small, must balance that bank to the penny every day. That's normal. Ask a nonbanker to suddenly do a bank-balancing job and he could suffer a little bit of a problem attempting it. For people in the newspaper and publishing business, putting the press to bed and meeting deadlines with copy is all in the day's work. But for an outsider it is something else.

As a manager, supervisor, or president would you raise productivity high where you are? Watch out for these *undue pressures* in jobs, senior and junior. Put fun, performance, profits in their place.

There are fifty headaches per person a year, your quota, medical experts say about our American population. "Some ten years ago twelve to fifteen million sleeping tablets were used to put the American people to sleep each night," says a drug company survey. The number of these tablets consumed has since increased 1,000 percent. We spend today 400 million dollars a year to buy headache-relieving pills.

We don't need to have all these headaches. Our answer is in what we do each day to see that our personal relations, our job relations, our customer relations are the best.

How do we make them the best? Get each person producing at his finest with customers, with associates? By meeting one of his most compelling desires!

V. *Security*—knowing he is performing

This security feeling is essential, but it needs to be *won* by what a person *does*. There is nothing more demoralizing than for an individual to knock himself out producing at full speed, then see a co-worker goofing off, sitting it out because "I've got tenure. They can't touch me. I'm just seven years away from my pension."

"In our company," said John Camp, production supervisor, "one *earns* security by putting out, not sitting out. But our people also know they are not working in an environment of pressure. If a person does not feel up to par physically, this is recognized and everything possible is done to help him return to health in cooperation with his doctor.

"One of the finest influences for performance in our business," Camp observed, "is to see people limited by a physical disability become some of our top producers. It is a challenge for them to win a game against odds, particularly when they know it means more pay, more opportunities and a wonderful feeling of security, knowing they *are* performing.''

Security Generates Profit Ideas

People whose minds are alert and confident with this sense of security often become *plus* performers by contributing many cost-saving profit ideas. Such creative talents can mean a double return for you as a manager.

Suppose your annual payroll is $100,000 and your profit margin is ten percent. One way you can earn $5,000 more profit is by getting $50,000 more sales. That's the hard way. An easy way is to reduce your costs five percent by increasing your productivity through cost-saving ideas. This five percent can be just a starter when you have at your command at least forty more cost-cutting ideas to capitalize on.

In the Fairfax Regulator Company where this kind of security is recognized throughout the organization, Rex Bell, president, suggested that each person in management arrange his schedule so that ''thirty minutes each day for a month, you get away from your desk and with paper and pencil zero in on ideas for saving costs and increasing profits in your operation.'' At the month's end, Bell asked them to share their ideas in discussion groups and consolidate them on chalkboards. They were then compared with a master cost-saving idea list gleaned from 22,000 managers from all types of companies who had participated in like discussions. The final product is ''Master Tool #2,'' pages 42-44.

Each manager used this master tool in working with his people and brought costs down company-wide more than seventeen percent. Benefits to the manager came in two ways: from the company's profit-sharing plan and recognition gained by increasing his own productivity record to a new high. These results were all generated in a climate of *security—because the individual knows he is performing*.

Begin tomorrow morning to tap the ''forty cost-saving ideas to profits'' (Master Tool #2) where you are, and watch costs go down, earnings up. Then score a double win by suggesting that your company incorporate this program in each department.

Now unleash the sixth desire, one of your most potent motivators for all-out performance.

VI. *Understanding* of his work, his business, what he makes possible for customers, his place in the organization

A major way to give him this fourfold understanding with one move is to link his ideas and everything he does to their effect on the customer. How do you do this?

When promising, aggressive graduates of the General Motors Institute come up with ideas for changing plant operations, supervisors often ask them, "Does it help sell the product?" This is the practical test.

The president of an established company, which was turned around from a loser to a profit winner, was asked, "What did it?" "A new look and understanding," he replied, "of each person's part in contributing to profitable customer business. No individual and no area of operation were taken for granted. As a result, the spirit of our organization is at its best because people see their place in the profit picture both for them and the company."

History shows twenty-one civilizations that have risen to the pinnacle of power, then have fallen and crashed. Each one fell because it failed to follow the gleam flowing from the throne of our Creator which reveals that each person is born with a thirst to understand, and to be understood, to see his place in the scheme of things.

How would you equip each person to produce at his best? Give him a complete understanding of (1) his job, (2) his business, (3) what he accomplishes for customers, (4) his place in the organization and what it means to him. Apply Key Two and you are sure of this result.

Master Tool #1

Trigger Six Tremendous Desires

    I. *Recognition* of each person as an individual making his own contribution.

    II. *Opportunity* for full use of his talents.

    III. *Seeing his place on the team*—he knows he fills a vital spot and management is counting on him.

    IV. *Enjoyment* of his work, his business, in congenial environment without *undue* pressures.

    V. *Security*—knowing he is performing.

    VI. *Understanding* of his work, his business, what he makes possible for customers, his place in the organization.

When you as a manager equip each individual to realize these six all-consuming desires, you turn on your greatest single motivating power to productivity and profits for him, for you, for your company.

Master Tool #2

Forty Sure Cost-Saving Ideas to Profits

Ways of Handling the Work

Look for the simplest way

Question need for each operation

Analyze, evaluate each job periodically for efficiency, wage determination, placement of people

Eliminate duplication

Use work simplification methods, motion study wherever practical

Establish best method and have all follow

Best working hours and conditions

Is more automation or mechanization needed?

Work Flow and Schedules

Investigate source of work to determine you are getting it at the best possible time

Be sure work is dispatched to others at the proper time

Plan for equipment and people for peak loads

Assign work equitably to right people
Avoid bottlenecks
Develop many job improvements

Equipment and Space

What is needed and where
Compare what you have with other available equipment that
  might be more advantageous
Lease or buy
Always compare cost with benefits to be derived
Watch changes in volume to determine effect on equipment
  needed
Look for new developments
Reduce material handling
Computerize routine work where practical
Inspect equipment regularly
Proper layout, space adequate, fully utilized, take advantage of
  specialization
Replacement rather than constant repair

Forms and Reports

Is form or report needed?
Can several forms be combined, simplified, standardized?
Eliminate paper—move faster what you have left

Controls

Clear, brief operating procedure for each job
—Keep up to date
Establish performance standards for each job
—Make sure they are reasonable and known
Frequent comparison of volume and personnel
—Quota control
—Never use four people when two can do the job
Control of quality, material, costs
Analyze work. Can it be done better in same amount of time?
Meet budget. Compare. Is it in line?
Responsibility fixed for all work done
Each person educated and trained to do his job right, know what is
  expected

Progress reports
Everyone on the job and using best tools
Check absenteeism, correct through individual discussions

Overall Points

Know each person, his qualities. Help him with his problems.
　Be alert to recommend promotions.
Suggestions: encourage, pay substantially, install, follow up
Plan ahead to avoid need for emergency action
"Auxiliary force" of help for peak periods and loads
Establish goals, known to each person, outline plans to reach,
　maintain a time schedule follow-up
Structure organization to meet problems of company
People placed to take advantage of their strong points, fairly
　appraised, equitably paid, incentive motivated
Reduce every problem you are trying to solve to the simplest
　possible terms
*Keep letting each individual know he has a personal stake in the
　everyday prosperity of your company*

KEY TWO

Triple Productivity
Through Know-Why
Know-How Power

To remain competitive, leaders in many companies are moving to meet this challenge:

Maximize your human resources. The real wealth of a business and a nation comes from the full productive use of the talents of your people.

How do you do this in your business and do it *now*? By capturing and putting to work quickly the world's greatest force.

"What is this force?" The know-why, know-how power of education and training.

"Where is it?" Right where you are, within the four walls of your company. No other power can match it.

"How do you begin?" Start this power flowing through your hands by answering these questions that person after person in each business is asking:

"What is my future here?"
"How far can I go?"
"What is expected of me on this job?"
"Where does it lead?"
"How can I make what I do count for the most?"

Equip each person with the know-why and know-how of his job, his business, what he makes possible for customers and his own advancement. When you do that you not only give him the answers he seeks, you make him one of your top producers. "The tragedy of modern times," says Sydney Harris, "can be summed up in the fact that we are developing large numbers of men and women who have the 'know-how' but pitifully few who have the 'know-why.' "

Give each one the "know-why" as well as the "know-how," and you unlock many unused productive talents he never knew he had. You do this through Key Two. This Key gives you a complete step-by-step program to triple the output of each person in your group. The steps start with chapter 3.

3

Threefold Education and Training Get Results

The secret of tripling the output of each person is in the base of your Triangle of Management.

"*My* Triangle of Management?"

As manager, supervisor, or president, you have three areas in which to gain or lose profits: operations, personal relations, and the know-why, know-how power of education and training, the base of this Management Triangle (see Master Tool #3). Without this base, the two sides of your Triangle, operations and personal relations, fall of their own weight. They stand up only because of this dynamic base which makes possible all-efficient operations, all-effective personal relations. At the Triangle's center is the customer, the only reason your company exists or that anyone has a job to do.

How well the operations of every department go depends completely on how well you deal with your people (personal relations) who make possible your operations. How well your operations, personal relations and customer relations go all hinge on how well you educate and train each person reporting to you.

At this point you may ask, "Why do you say, 'education *and* training?' Why not just 'training?' "

Training alone will never do it.

To know and understand the goals of any business, its products and services, and the individual's part in producing these products

TRIANGLE OF MANAGEMENT

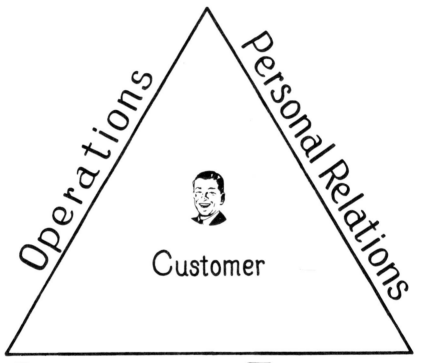

Operations

Personal Relations

Customer

Education and Training
Know-Why   *Know-How*

MANAGEMENT

INDIVIDUAL JOBS

CUSTOMER RELATIONS

and services for the customer *is education.* To learn how to do work
assignments in that business *is training.*

Education the Know-Why—Training the Know-How

Any person, senior or junior, can have all the know-how there
is, but unless he has the know-why and the motivation that goes
with it, he accomplishes little for himself or his business. This know-
why relates each job in the company to the broad picture of "why"
these jobs are, the relation of each to the others, and the place of
each job and each individual performing his job in bringing about
the end result—the services and products to meet the needs of more
and more customers at a profit.

The know-why is the heartbeat of your business, its reason for
being. It is the *Dominant Idea* (see Chapter 1). It is your company's
exciting future.

The Life Blood of Your Business
Flows Through Three Arteries

Electronics, food, steel, publishing, plastics, banking, your business,
whether it has a few people or thousands, pours its energies through
three main arteries: operations, personal relations, education and training. Your success and that of each person reporting to you all depend
on your putting the *motivating know-why* into each of these arteries
with your people each business day. What you do in these three areas
of responsibility makes you a *whole* manager, a winning manager,
shapes your future and that of each person in your group.

"But my managing job," you say, "is still an operating job—to
get out the work, produce quality services and products at competitive
costs. I haven't time to educate and train. Sure I need to get a lot
more work out of people, cut my high-cost payroll dollars. But, look
at my desk! I'm snowed under. When am I going to find the time
to educate and train people?"

Here is where your use of the base of the Management Triangle
not only *gives* you that time but multiplies it through the people around
you. Multiply yourself through others! How? By tapping their many
unused talents to take over that work piled on your desk, show what

they can do with it and free you for managing and teaching which is your key to moving ahead far and fast.

Tap these unused talents on your payroll with three steps:

1. Equip each person to operate at his top job performance
2. Develop managers and future managers to back you up
3. Win more and more customers in six key ways

The step-by-step procedure in these three actions to get the results you want is visualized in the next three chapters.

- Would you like to get out from under the pile on your desk?
- Put fun into your job?
- Triple individual productivity?
- Increase profits for your department and company?
- Cut rising costs?
- Open up new roads in advancement and earning power for you and those working with you?

The chapters ahead show specific sure ways to realize these goals *now*.

4

Equip Each Person for Top Job Performance

> "Bob Rand, this is Gregg Swanson," said the personnel manager of Barden Communications to the operating supervisor. "Gregg has just come with us, as you know. Will you show him his job?"
>
> "Glad to have you aboard, Gregg," said Rand as they sat down. "Why don't you read this operating manual [handing him a book three inches thick]. It will tell you all about it, while I get caught up with my work."

What an introduction to a new job and career which Gregg Swanson had been looking forward to with enthusiasm. Now he was ready to walk out of the place. This kind of an introduction, which will be his only "training," is going on at hundreds of companies this minute. Thirty years of examining the education and training programs of companies from coast to coast shows this incident to be *normal* procedure in business after business. Less than one out of five companies in this nation have any formalized training. As a result, turnover of people is one of today's costliest drains on the profit dollar. Thirty percent turnover is low. In factories, up to fifty percent is common.

How to Cut This Turnover in Half

You can stop this drain, change expense dollars into profit dollars for you and your company by one quick action:

51

MOVE ONE:
INTRODUCTORY PROGRAM

Recommend and initiate the "Three-Part Introductory Program" set forth in Master Tool #4 below. Companies using it have reduced turnover by fifty percent and more.

Master Tool #4

Three-Part Introductory Program
Reduces Turnover by Half

Introduction to Your Company

How it started and how it grew.
Its position today. Its place in our community.
The people and industry it serves.
How it is expanding. New markets.
How your company is organized, its structure, management, goals.
Your products and services.
Each person's part in making possible these products and services.
Importance of customer relations. New business efforts on each job.
Your company's practices and procedure affecting each person.
Company benefits to you: incentive plans, profit sharing, retirement, insurance, illness, vacations, safety and health.
Opportunities and advantages of a career with your company.
Channels of promotion, salary and wage progression, specific education and training programs, tuition refund plan.
Personal qualities needed for advancement.
Personal guided tour of company and its operations.

Introduction to Your Department and Section

Departmental activities and functions.
Interrelations with other departments and company.
Introduction to each person in management.
Introduction to each of your associates.
Personal tour of department, its operation and facilities, including lounge, luncheon, and refreshments.

Introduction to Your Job

Complete step-by-step, on-the-job education and training, visualizing the purpose of the job, its relation to other jobs, just what it accomplishes for customers.
Your exact position in the entire organization.

NEW STAFF
(ex-Personnel Dept.)

SUPERVISORS REPRESENT MANAGEMENT!!

Good Supervision	Bad Supervision
1. "Welcome to the team"	1. A surly welcome
2. "What the department does"	2. Find out yourself
3. Personal introduction to other staff	3. Find out yourself
4. Department's organization chart	4. Find out yourself
5. How department interrelates (with other departments)	5. Find out yourself
6. Assignment and responsibility to RELIABLE Staff Member	6. No assignment
7. Brief job description	7. No job description
8. Reassurance	8. Indifference
9. Criticism	9. No criticism
10. Praise	10. Indifference
11. 1st Month Evaluation—explained!	11. 1st Month Evaluation—not explained
12. 2nd Month Evaluation—explained!	12. 2nd Month Evaluation—not explained
13. 3rd Month Evaluation—explained!	13. 3rd Month Evaluation—not explained
14. Personal recommendation—permanent staff	14. Indifference
15. Interview with Department Head	15. No interview
16. Interview with Manager	16. No interview
17. Reasonable potential good impression	17. Frustration, boredom, indifference and LOST

DIPLOMACY, TACT, IMPARTIALITY, FRIENDLINESS, CONSIDERATION, CRITICISM & PRAISE ARE "MUSTS."

---

† Courtesy of the Bank of N.T. Butterfield & Son Ltd., Bermuda.

"It's hard to believe, but for forty years we were without such a program," said the general manager of a leading utilities company. "A year ago we put it into operation with the latest information and newest techniques, and it has already cut our turnover in two."

It does more than that. Companies whose people become high producers find this orientation procedure essential in visualizing to each person his part in achieving the major goals of the organization and the specific opportunities offered him for advancement and profit if he performs.

How to Dramatize It

Make your introductory presentation "come alive" at the start by getting your president to be on the spot to greet each new person and to tell about his job. It will be an eye opener to them. Use video tapes, films, transparencies, live demonstrations and panel discussions to visualize your products and services, new markets being opened, techniques to win new customers, and career opportunities.

Usually the industrial relations or personnel department conducts the "Introduction to your company." Supervisors or managers take over the "Introduction to your department or section" and the "Introduction to your job." Should you have experienced people without this basic information about their company and their jobs, here is the chance to give it to them at the time the program is started. It can raise their performance to major proportions. *Without it, they cannot possibly do superior work.*

If you would make a move that will have far-reaching results, suggest this three-part introduction program to your company, offer to help get it started. Two profit gains are sure to follow: costly turnover down, productivity sharply up.

Why do most companies miss on this big profit earner? Because everyone is too busy with other things, running from one problem to another—production, sales, finances. No one person comes up for air, takes time to take hold of this sure-fire productivity winner, get it going in his company. Be sure of this: nothing happens until some one individual with imagination and the know-why, know-how of what to do with a profit idea *makes* it happen. Be that person and be out in front both in your company and with your competitors.

The Supervisor Is the Key to Slashing Turnover Costs

The supervisor *is* the company. How he uses Master Tool #4 makes its success. This is dramatically shown in Exhibit A, page 53.

MOVE TWO:
VISUALLY ANALYZE EACH JOB
FOR PROFIT

You are ready at this point to make the second of five profit moves to prepare each person quickly to produce at his best (Master Tool #5, page 63).

To do his best work each individual wants answers to these questions about his job:

What is the objective?
What does it accomplish?
How is it related to other jobs?
How is my job done and why?
What is expected of me?

Giving him clear answers is essential to superior production. The visual analysis of a job not only answers these questions but accomplishes six major results for you and your company.

1. Establishes the objective and standard of performance for the job.
2. Reduces the initial break-in time for new people by fifty percent or more.
3. Increases the performance of experienced people.
4. Uncovers new and improved ways to do the job.
5. Combines the operating procedure and teaching program for the job into this one brief, time-saving document.
6. Eliminates lengthy, complicated procedures and manuals and time to keep them up to date.

Replace Confusion with Simplicity

One of the high costs in business today is time and interest lost through confusion of many people about their jobs. New people try to learn their jobs and experienced people try to carry on with nothing in writing or with long, wordy, technical instructions which confuse even the experts.

The Ten Commandments took 298 words. The Declaration of Independence took 286 words. Lincoln's Gettysburg Address took just 271 words, while an order to reduce the price of cabbage coming out of the Price Stabilization Office, when we had it, took 29,411 words.

Too many companies attempt to use bulky operating procedures and training manuals which they find impossible to keep up to date. Other companies have nothing in writing, attempt to operate "off the cuff" by word of mouth. Here is where the ball is easily dropped, and costly errors made. Yet they find reducing operations to writing is too difficult and time consuming. What is the answer? The Visual Analysis technique.

The Visual Analysis Technique—
What It Is and Will Do for You

A visual analysis is a word photograph of a job. It is made up of just four simple elements: (1) Standard of Performance, (2) Objective, (3) Job Factors, (4) Key Points. It is a telegraphic word picture of the factors which make up the job from the first to the last step in sequence of operation. The key points are the points which get the job factor accomplished. This word picture becomes the official procedure to operate by and to teach by for every person performing that job.

This book contains five visual analyses of key jobs in every business, which, in the hands of each officer, manager, supervisor, sales and customer relations person, can triple productivity, cut rising costs, up earnings, attract more business each day.

They are:

These visual procedures can be just the start. Each of your jobs written in this way can bring you equal productivity gains.

How to Set Up Simply

Using these examples you can quickly prepare a visual analysis for *any* job, senior or junior. Writing the procedure can easily be done by experienced people on the job with the help of the supervisor. Doing it will uncover major cost savings and job improvements to increase individual output.

When writing up the job, keep asking these questions:

—Is there a better, simpler way to do it?
—Can I eliminate a factor completely?
—Is it necessary?
—Can I combine certain factors?
—Is my time organized well to do the job?
—Is it scheduled right?
—Am I delayed in getting work to others?
—Is work flow coming to me at the proper time?
—Is time being wasted at any point?
—Do I have all information to best do the job?

Standard of Performance Gives Great Advantage

To find this standard, apply an established work measurement formula if your company has one. If not, take the peaks and valleys of production on that job. A standard of performance should reflect a fair average of these ups and downs in a day's work or a week's work for each person. This fair average should be established by a study of this volume over a sufficient representative period of time to give you the standard of performance for that job.

Place this standard at the top of each job procedure. It will prove to be highly effective in raising each individual's output. Explain what reaching the standard can do for him in promotion and advancement, and encourage his questions.

This program will raise individual output wherever applied. The president of a twenty-store chain of food markets finds that his biggest overall savings in productivity come in setting standards of performance on every job. "Our people know exactly what they should do from the time they get into the store to the time they leave."

A leader in the management consulting field has lifted its productivity thirty percent on routine projects alone by establishing performance standards and showing each person on the job just what is expected of him and what attaining these standards means to him.

Removing Blocks to High Output

For many people who are producing less than normal (100 percent standard of performance), it is because of one or more of these causes:

1. Lack of work or unequal distribution of work
2. Change of operation
3. Individual's attitude toward the work
4. Inadequate education (know-why) and training (know-how) for the job
5. Job placement problem

When you deal with these causes promptly and correct them, the person in practically every instance attains his standard and with it a satisfaction of achievement he has never felt before.

MOVE THREE:
APPLY THE SIX STEPS
TO SUCCESSFUL TEACHING

With the visual analysis operating procedure for the job as your teaching agenda, start preparing the new person to take hold of his new job with confidence by your use of the six sure teaching steps,

Master Tool #12, page 108. The value of its use is brought out fully in Key Three, chapter 7.

Where Productivity and Profits Get Away

It is at this point that nine out of ten companies let productivity and profits slip through their fingers. All the person learning the new job has to help him is a "catch as catch can" explanation at the best, which leaves him empty-handed and frustrated. His only alternative is to break himself in under a "sink or swim" situation. It is anything but the way to win, but it happens regularly because the manager or supervisor responsible does not know about these sure teaching steps. Now you have them, and with them the six supporting principles to make your teaching doubly effective. (See chapter 7, pages 101 to 107.)

Equipped with these tools you can be the most productive teacher in your company, far better than any college professor from the outside. Why? Because you *know your business* and this can be your greatest asset. You have *lived* it. You have the answers to give to the person you are teaching, which he must have to compete.

Value of Cassette Tape Programmed Instruction

When you need to teach, for high productivity results, the know-why, know-how of their jobs to a large group of persons doing similar work, cassette tape programmed instruction may be your answer. What is it? It is preparing instruction on tapes in "cassette" form, to be run on a recorder which the individual at his own speed synchronizes with his accompanying instruction manual.

For example, banks which handle a heavy volume of security transactions for customers find this teaching technique very effective. Separate tape cassettes are prepared with interrelated manuals picturing the step-by-step handling of specific types of stock and bond transactions. Jobs clearly dramatized in this way include paying dividends and interest, security descriptions, identifying a negotiable security, assignment of securities, and the use of nominees. Actual conversations with the customer in handling particular transactions with dispatch are part of the taped course.

Should you wish to apply this technique to volume jobs in your organization, leading companies which make cassette tape recorders can show you how to build your own job instruction courses.

Programmed Instruction without Tapes

You can simplify the teaching of many people doing the same volume job by writing a manual in "programmed instruction style," a do-it-yourself type of education and training. This instruction permits each person to work by himself at his own pace. Large mail order houses have, for example, such a self-learning course on "writing customer orders," which has raised individual performance substantially.

However, programmed instruction with or without tape cassettes is suggested only as an alternative to personal face-to-face teaching where large groups of people must be taught similar volume jobs and the time saved is at a high premium. Job education and training have benefited not only from programmed instruction, but from audio-visual and other media, including teaching machines, and closed-circuit television. But there is no substitute for the effectiveness of individual person-to-person instruction based on the six steps to successful teaching.

MOVE FOUR:
GAIN PROFITS BY
KEEPING TO SCHEDULE

How much time you take with the individual for each teaching step depends on the nature of the job and the person being taught. Tailor the time to fit the job and the individual. Avoid losing continuity by letting time lapse unduly between the steps. Guard against ever postponing the breaking-in process. To permit a person to be on the job *unprepared* is a sure way to invite costly mistakes affecting both customers and profits.

Adequate Teaching Is a Big Cost Saver

Keep before you the fact that it takes far less time to promptly apply the six steps to successful teaching than it does to try to straighten out profit-robbing errors made by a person tragically unequipped.

MOVE FIVE:
KNOW AND TALK WITH EACH PERSON

"This is my ace move to get high individual productivity," said Barry Gardner, outstanding supervisor for the rapidly expanding Grant Marketing Research Corporation. "Jim Bates, age 17, a school dropout working with our group, asked me what he accomplished by standing eight hours a day collating papers. I sat down with him, explained the whole process, how these papers go through two main offices and one branch office, then to our field man sitting in some grocery store in Texas filling out this form; how he sends it back to us, and if Jim doesn't collate it right or accidentally loses a sheet, how it is possible to lose a client worth thousands of dollars.

"Our discussions changed Jim's whole outlook on his job and his career. His performance moved from substandard to superior. He is taking a correspondence course to get his high school diploma, and his promotion road ahead is wide open.

"This is just one of many experiences that prove to me that if you care enough to help people get ahead, it is well worth talking with them two or three times a week."

Managers who *know and talk with each person* gain high productivity three ways: for the individual, the company, and his own production record.

Performance Clues

There are clues to stepping up individual performance, gleaned from these conversations, that the other four moves may never uncover. The questions below have come out of thousands of interviews conducted by managers in many fields. The right answers to them have proved to be the *key* to causing the individual to go all-out in his work. Only by living close to his people, helping them with work problems, being acquainted with their situation, their strong points and the qualities which need strengthening, can the manager have *the answer* which moves people to produce at their best.

Answers to these questions are crucial:

—"Where can I improve?" (An honest evaluation of his work)
—"What are my chances for promotion?"

—"How secure is my position?"

—"Where are the lines of promotion and opportunities so I can see where I fit in and where I can go?"

—"How much can I earn on this job? How far can I go?"

—"What are company plans for increasing business and profits?"

—"What changes in operations and policies are planned?"

—"What effect will it have on me?"

—"How can I make myself more valuable?"

—"Do I fit into future plans?"

—"What can I do to contribute to the company's expansion, growth and well being?"

—"If I put out with this added effort how will I benefit?"

This positive reaction coming out of these thousands of day-to-day interviews is typical: "My manager cares enough about me and my future to take time to talk with me. This makes me want to really put out for that guy."

Five Moves to High Productivity Make the Job Fun

"When I wasn't doing what I knew I could do, playing baseball wasn't fun," said a .384 major league hitting star the other day. "Now I am doing what I know I can do and the game is fun." His fun began when he decided to give up the idea he could hit home runs and began to concentrate on shortening his batting stroke and stride, making contact and picking good pitches.

These techniques for doing what he knows he can do *are in business the five moves* winning managers find bring fun and high productivity to their people on job after job. Begin using them now where you are. Don't worry about getting all five going. Just start with the moves *you know you can make*. Each one contains the power to raise individual performance to new highs. Using all five gives you a king size production arsenal. This arsenal is a gold mine for you. Tap it!

Master Tool #5

Prepare Each Person for High Productivity
Make Five Moves

1. Fully introduce (orient) new and experienced people to company, department, job. Reduce turnover by half. (Master Tool #4)
2. Make visual analysis operating procedure for each job to operate by and teach by. Realize major cost savings. (Page 56)
3. Use the six steps to successful teaching. (Master Tool #12, and Key Three, Chapter 7)
4. Secure profits by keeping to schedule.
5. Know and talk with each person. Show him what his job means to customer and his own advancement.

5

Develop Managers and
Future Managers <u>Now</u>

Do you have your own back-up ready to take your place so you can move up quickly? Your company looks to you to prepare your own successor. And if management sees you have no one or finds him unqualified, the chances are great you will stay stymied where you are and watch another individual, who does have his replacement ready, grab that opportunity you have set your sights on.

Preparing his own back-up is a hallmark of the manager who is a high producer, a high profit maker. It is a crucial test being used by the company which is out in front. Why? Projections show that within the ten years immediately ahead of us, *one-half* of the executives in our companies will have successors in their places. Not only that but expansion will bring a fifty percent increase in new managerial openings *over and above man-for-man replacement*.

Will you be ready, will each promoted officer, manager or supervisor be able to take advantage of these multiplying new responsibilities? You can be sure you will be when you are equipped to answer the eight questions in Master Tool #6, page 68. A company's profits and growth will climb only as long as leaders in each area of the business answer these questions with positive, aggressive action.

How does each one do this? In the four ways listed below.

I. Develops himself

He uses the "Eight Session Management Course," Master Tool #7, page 69, as a self-check list. His answers to the eight questions are in the subjects and tools brought out in each Key and chapter of this book.

II. Helps establish the eight session course in the company—participates in it

The course is designed so that you can make it do quickly two things for you: (1) a seminar course for seasoned officers, managers, supervisors or foremen, (2) a course to equip new and potential managers and supervisors who are suddenly needed to fill openings due to emergencies, changes and expansion.

Such a program, run on company time, one hour a week or as you decide, with company officers participating to give it authority and standing, can be your most important single move for your own future and the future of your company. Coordinate the course through the company's industrial relations or personnel officer, rotating the leaders of the eight sessions among the best qualified people. Get individuals throughout the organization helping with ideas to insure its wide acceptance. Then make sure that the course is periodically rescheduled to meet changing problems and opportunities, to boost job performance, to sell many more of your products and services, to win a host of new customers.

III. Develops his own back-up—sees that he takes part in course

Each key person, if he is to move and go far, needs to prepare the individual coming up behind him. This means equipping that person to develop himself while participating in and contributing to the success of this course.

IV. Inspires people in his group with the knowledge that each one has a contribution to make no one else can make

Build in each person the idea that he is made for success, that he has only begun to tap the possibilities within him. Let him see that you are here to help him go just as far as his developing abilities will take him.

"You are you. Each person is different from every other person anywhere. You have your own individual contribution to make on your job to both your own and the company's advancement. If you don't make it, it will never be made." Uncover this contribution in the wealth of ideas and actions contained in the Five Keys to Productivity and Profits. Then use it to bring about three goals: raise individual performance high; reduce rising costs; accelerate earnings. Gain these three objectives and your rise as a manager can be rapid and rewarding. Build solidly on these talents by making the moves developed in the next chapter.

Master Tool #6

HOW DO YOU ANSWER THESE KEY QUESTIONS?

Your Decisions Are Rooted in Eight People Areas

Triangle of Management

1. How do we expand our products, services, markets, win customers in fast competition?

2. Have we back-ups for key jobs, flexibility for growth, for sudden organization changes?

3. Where are we in research, long-range planning?
   Where will our company be, our markets, our jobs in five years?

4. How do we increase profits, reduce costs?

5. How do we recruit, develop enthusiastic, high-producing company staff?

6. How do we best administer salaries, wages, other financial incentives?
   Are our programs adequate for appraising each person, evaluating each job, promoting people?
   Are pension, profit-sharing, benefit provisions competitive?

7. How do we build SPIRIT, motivation throughout our company?
   How sharp are our communications with each company person, directors, customers, stockholders, the community we serve?

8. Do we have complete, specific education and training programs in job performance, management development, sales, customer and public relations?

A VITAL, EASILY APPLIED PROGRAM
FOR A GROWING COMPANY

Eight Session Management Course

Session 1

Key Question: Have we back-ups for key jobs? Have we flexibility for growth and for sudden organizational changes?

What constitutes our job of managing?
Developing people is our most important assignment.
Tapping our deepest unused reservoir.

Manager or supervisor has just three responsibilities: operations, personal relations, education and training—the three sides of the triangle of management.

Three-point program to (1) develop managers, leaders, teachers; (2) equip each person for best job performance; (3) win many customers in specific key ways.

How to lighten your management load, achieve top operations, and enthusiastic personal relations.

Session 2

Key Question: Where are we in long-range planning? Where will our department, our company, our jobs, our markets be in five years?

What qualities make a manager?

Imagination to plan ahead.

Multiplying yourself through others.

Assigning responsibilities to people only after developing them.

What delegating work means.

The essential follow-up process.

Session 3

Key Question: How can we expand our products, services, and markets to win customers in fast competition?

Personalize everything we do. Visualize everything we do.

Get everyone participating.

Every member a salesman for the company, winning customers by:
(1) knowing our products and services
(2) dealing with customers face to face
(3) using the telephone effectively
(4) writing productive letters
(5) handling customer's business right "behind the scenes"
(6) working with community groups

Get hold of the dominant idea that builds and makes our company.

Inspire each person by showing what he accomplishes for customers and his own advancement through his own efforts.

Session 4

Key Question: How do we increase profits, reduce costs?

Where do earnings come from? Where do profits come from?

Chief sources to tap.

Reduce costs through improving methods:
Full and efficient use of each person's time by study of operating procedure for each job to determine best method by considering:
ways of handling the work
work flow and schedules
equipment
forms and reports
space
controls
suggestions

Make visual analysis on individual jobs to accomplish six major cost savings for you:
Establish objective and standard of performance for each job.
Reduce initial education and training (break-in) time fifty percent or more for each person on a new job.
Increase the job performance of experienced people.
Uncover new and improved ways to do the job.
Combine operating procedure and teaching program in one brief document.
Eliminate lengthy, complicated procedures and manuals, and time to keep them up to date.

Session 5

> *Key Question: How can we recruit and develop enthusiastic, high producing people in each department?*

You *are* the Personnel Department where you are.

Building our company, our unit around people.

Effective personal relations embraces five areas of activity:
(1) Selection and employment
(2) Placement, promotion, salary and wage progress
(3) Security, both physical and mental
(4) Social and recreational activities
(5) Communications and community relations

Session 6

> *Key Question: How can we best administer salaries and wages and other financial compensations? Are our programs adequate for appraising each person, evaluating each job, and promoting people? Are pension, profit sharing, and insurance provisions competitive?*

Recruiting, selecting, placing, promoting.

Evaluating people and jobs; relation to advancement, salary and wage progress, effectiveness of our products and services.

Periodic appraisals of each person.

Scheduled discussions with each individual.
Let each one know what is expected of him and how he is doing.
Give recognition when due.
Tell person in advance about changes that affect him.
Make best use of each person's ability for job satisfaction.

Session 7

> *Key Question: How can we build spirit and motivation throughout our department and company? How sharp are our communications with each person on the job, with associates, directors, customers, stockholders, and the community we serve?*

You *are* the company to each person. What you do builds or destroys enthusiasm for his job.

What factors build *spirit* in an organization?

How can we motivate people to do their best job perform-ance?

Tapping immense unused talents within you and your people.

Communication techniques for maximum productive effort and job satisfaction.

Working effectively with others. How to work with superiors. How to work with associates.

Session 8

> *Key Question: Do we have complete education and train-ing programs in (1) job performance; (2) management development; (3) sales, cus-tomer and public relations?*

Your vital place in the education and training process.

Specific program for introducing and orienting new people to company, department, and job. Company organization, his-tory, place in community, wide scope of products or services, what each person accomplishes for customers. Opportunities, advantages of, and qualifications for a business career.

Future of company hinges on each management person being a teacher.

Six sure steps to successful teaching. Arrange time and sched-ule.

How to conduct effective staff meetings and group discussions.

Five steps to profitable selling inside and out.

6

Open Doors to a New World of Customers

This chapter uncovers a powerful generator to people-productivity and profits. A tragic mistake is being made in many businesses with the most precious person in our economy—the customer. He is at the center of the Triangle of Management (Master Tool #3, page 48). *Without him* no business can survive, no jobs can exist. None of us has a future or a country. *With him* the road ahead can be wide open.

What is this mistake? Turning loose employees, senior and junior, to deal with customers and prospects without giving them specific education and training in the know-why, know-how to cause each customer to say enthusiastically to himself, "This is where I like to do business." It is at this point of customer contact that productivity and profits are either going down the drain in big chunks or are moving you and your company far ahead of your competitors. Which is it?

These current experiences, lifted from more than 8,000 personal incidents, dramatize a major success key:

Aspen, Colorado—at a nationally known gas station

Gordon: "How do I get to Estes Park from here?"
Gas station manager: "I don't know. I've never been there. I don't have my glasses, so I can't show you any way on the map. And I don't have a map."

Same day—Colorado Springs, leading merchandising store

Aliff and Gordon are going through the stock on the counters, looking over the kind of blankets we want up in our mountain cabins. An exceptionally competent sales lady, while waiting on another customer notices us looking for the blankets we want. With a vibrant voice and an attractive smile, she says to us: "We've got terrific bargain buys in blankets today. Let me show you where they are." Points to them and says, "I'll be with you in a moment." Completes sale with customer she is serving, then, "Now let me tell you about them. . . ."
Aliff: "This is just what we want. We would like four blankets. Thank you very much. You're right on the ball."

How to Lose Customers by Telephone

Customer calling officer of public relations firm

Customer:	"Mr. Rex Gabbit, please."
Office person:	"Mr. Gabbit isn't available now."
Customer:	"When will he be available?"
Office person:	"I don't know because his secretary is in a meeting and she is not available."
Customer:	"When will she be out?"
Office person:	"I don't know. She didn't tell me. If you'll leave your number, when they're available, I'll ask one of them to call you."

How to Win Customers by Telephone

Same day—Customer calling president of brokerage firm

Customer:	"I'd like to speak with Mr. John Crayden."
Answering, first ring:	"This is John Crayden."
Customer, surprised:	"Mr. Crayden, I'm Gordon Blake. You really gave me a shock. When I call most companies, after waiting for an answer, I go through a

	receptionist, and a secretary before finally getting my man. You're amazing!"
Crayden:	"Well, Mr. Blake, our practice is for everyone to answer his own phone whenever possible. We find that this kind of person-to-person contact means a lot to our clients. Now, how can I help you?"

Whole New World of Customers to Tap

Are you and each one around you prepared to go after these vast new markets?

—Customers across this nation are being lost this minute because people, senior and junior, are sadly unequipped for contact relationships whether face to face, over the telephone, or by letter.

—Fifteen million new family units will be formed in this decade, generating multiple demands for your services or products. On top of these needs will be calls from millions of established families moving into higher earnings.

—*Every day* nearly 10,000 babies are born, ushering in a whole set of new needs to be filled. Over 10,000 young persons turn 21, and over 4,000 men and women cross the mysterious line labeled age 65. Each 24 hours there are over 5,000 marriages and about 1,500 divorces. Each month the mail brings a social security check to 24 million beneficiaries.

—One out of every five families move to a new community every year. Are you getting your share of these new customers? Just to keep even every business has to add new accounts every year to replace the business that's lost naturally when people move or die.

Make sure you have the competitive edge by giving every contact individual the specific know-why, know-how of attracting customers in five key ways.

Winning Techniques Must Be Taught

Winning techniques do not just happen. People in a myriad of contact positions, without the kind of specific know-why, know-how education and training contained in these pages, will go right along alienating customers at countless points. Many of these customers can be yours if you are ready. To win them and a host of others who are part of this world of expanding new markets calls for quickly putting to work where you are the following five vital programs.

I. Know your products and services. Be alert to suggest them to many people. Fit them to their needs.

To get ideas to introduce your teaching of this key way listen to a top level conversation.

"To make profits, concentrate on selling more and more quality products and services at competitive costs," said the president of a fast-growing conglomerate organization.

"Those profits will soon disappear, John, the moment you stop meeting and creating people needs," replied the head of a leading merchandising company.

He called the shot perfectly. Within two years the *profit-minded-only* business was in financial trouble. The merchandising company is having record growth, and its earnings position is stronger than ever.

The Key Is to Meet and Create NEEDS at a Profit

You do this by constantly improving your products and services and creating new ones. Make sure your people *know* what these are and what they will do for customers. To accomplish this goal, companies often run quiz contests with first, second, and third place prizes, including all-expenses-paid trips abroad, and extra vacation time.

There is nothing that will attract customers to you faster than to go out of your way to fit your products to their needs. You will enjoy this great competitive advantage only when you *know* these services and are quick to bring them to the customer's attention.

II. Sell customers face to face—inside and out

Your know-why, know-how program for selling person-to-person can take these three moves:

1. A top company in the financial field starts equipping each customer-contact person in this way:

    a. What do our customers want when they walk through the revolving door? What do they expect from us? They expect:
    1. efficiency, courtesy, and very fast service
    2. information on our services
    3. to be made to feel important

Our customer expects these things regardless of how he behaves. He may be really nasty and spoiling for a fight. However you mustn't be the one who gives it to him. There are two reasons. The obvious and rather selfish consequence is that he may report you to your supervisor. The second and most important reason is that he is a customer who deserves our best attitudes and treatment. We must be gracious to all customers, regardless of their behavior, or their appearance.

    b. We know it's never safe to judge anyone by his looks. The other day one of the largest purchases of traveler's checks in history was made by a little man who was most unpleasant to deal with. He never changed his clothes, rarely shaved, and bought $20.00 worth of traveler's checks every two weeks. One day, after a number of years in the U.S., he came in and bought between $100,000 and $200,000 worth of checks. He was planning to return to his native South America, and he chose to take his life savings in that form. No one ever would have been able to tell from his appearance that he had that much money.

    c. *You use seventy-two muscles to frown—only fourteen to smile.* Smiling is less work and more fun, and the greatest pulling magnet to win customers you will ever have going for you. Yet you find less than one percent of those in public contact positions with any semblance of a smile on their faces. Most of them think they are smiling when they're not. Smiling takes a lot of practice for most people.

2. With every business facing the keenest competition, each person needs to be a salesman for his company, whatever his job may be. Selling in specific ways and at every opportunity can mean many more customers, and advancement in position and income for the person who does it. He is selling each time he deals with a customer or prospect face to face, answers a telephone, writes a letter, makes or handles a product or service "behind the scenes." But it is in

face-to-face selling inside and outside your place of business where one of the most vital impacts on productivity, profits and growth happens daily.

3. You can prepare each individual for selling at counters, desks, and windows by taking Master Tool #8, "Productive Selling Face to Face," pages 81-86, and hold three one-hour group discussions covering the thirteen job factors with their key points. Then place this Master Tool in each person's hands to use and refer to daily. It can lift their selling performance to new highs.

Be sure to encourage each one to clear any questions with his supervisor or manager as soon as opportunity affords, so that he handles each customer with confidence.

Five-Step Selling Inside and Out

These are the steps used with premium results by top salesmen in every product and service field. They are set forth in Master Tool #9, "Five-Step Productive Selling—Inside and Out, pages 87-89. Hold two one-hour group discussions using this Master Tool as your teaching agenda, then put this Master Tool in the hands of each person who is selling either outside your place of business or inside, and watch your sales mount.

III. Answer the telephone to win

There are over 300 million telephone calls a day in the United States alone. Telephoning is big business. Each time we pick up that company phone, what we say and how we say it can quickly win or lose customers.

Use just four simple essentials. They come out of more than thirty-five years of research and continuous day-to-day observations. They are recommended by telephone companies the world over. Take Master Tool #10, "Answering the Telephone to Win," pages 90-93, and conduct four one-hour sessions, using this Master Tool as your discussion agenda. Then place the Tool in the possession of every person to apply with each telephone conversation.

IV. Write productive letters

The post office of one major city alone handles more than twelve million letters a day. Letters well written build good relations for every growing company. Each letter is our personal calling card. It represents us and our company. When it is on its way to the customer we can not call it back. It is gone and with it our reputation and that of our organization.

To multiply the letter-writing talents of each person, regularly use "The Four C's" Master Tool #11, "Four Tests for Effective Letters." Arrange for each one who dictates, writes or signs letters to participate in four group discussions, with each of the "Four C's" the subject for one of the four sessions.

One very effective way to secure material for these sessions is to make an extra copy of each letter received and answered over a two- or three-week period, then rewrite your answers for certain letters, testing them against the "Four C's." Throw the most striking "before and after" letters on the screen through an opaque projector, deleting any identifying signatures, and give each discussion participant the benefits of each point visualized.

Give each person Master Tool #11, "Four Tests for Effective Letters" to use daily as he writes, dictates or signs one of the most potent mediums for winning or losing customers.

V. Tell your business story throughout the community

You may be doing this telling function now in a very complete way. Studies show, however, that the lack of an *understanding* of many individual industries, products and services and what they will do to meet a whole range of needs, is widespread. One of the surest means of getting your company's unique message across to every corner of your market is by members of your organization speaking effectively before schools, clubs, civic and business groups, on radio and television. Each member of management can do this important job by reading and studying Chapter 8, "Speak with Force—You

Can Do It," pages 115-123, and applying Master Tool #13, page 123, "Use These Six Principles to Make Your Speaking Outstanding."

The ability to speak well with any size group should be a part of the equipment of every executive. We live in a fast-moving world where ideas and information need to be conveyed widely at every opportunity. No key person—and you are just that—can afford to be in the awkward position of feeling ill at ease when called upon to speak to any audience. Nor should one ever need to be in that position when these sure public speaking principles are available to you.

They are principles that win audiences. They have been tested through the white heat of more than six thousand personal experiences and through studying a host of speakers in action. What one does with those principles can mean the difference between speaking poorly and the frustration that goes with it, and speaking with power and enjoying the knowledge that you have scored with your audience.

This move is suggested. It works. Develop the fine speaking talents through the six principles which make a speaker outstanding and encourage others to develop them. By so doing you will put in your hands a powerful public relations weapon which your competitors will be without unless they make this same move.

Doorways to Productivity and Growth

If you are acting on each page of this chapter, you are opening wide these five doorways to rich new business areas:

—Know your products and services. Be alert to suggest them to many people. Fit them to their needs.
—Sell customers face to face—inside and out.
—Answer the telephone to win.
—Write productive letters.
—Tell your business story throughout the community.

Turn now to Key Three, the next step to record productivity and profits for you and people working with you.

Master Tool #8

**Productive Selling Face to Face
At Counters, Desks and Windows**

*Visual Analysis
Operating Procedure*

Standard of Performance

1. Give efficient, courteous, very fast service.
2. Have customer leave with enthusiastic feeling, "I'm glad I came here."
3. Be alert for new business. Make the sale if in the best interests of customer.

Objective: To help person coming to see us do what he wants to do, and to fit our products or services to his needs.

Use imagination at every point to accomplish this goal.

Job Factors	*Key Points*
1. Quickly welcome an approaching customer pleasantly and courteously.	a. Develop the knack of looking up from your work when a customer approaches or is at your desk or counter.
	b. Go out of your way to greet a customer, welcome him with a smile and greet him by name if you can.
	c. Treat him as you would a guest coming into your home; make him feel at ease.
	d. Be alert to people waiting for attention and inquire if you may help.
	e. Take the initiative, don't wait for him to wonder

Job Factors	*Key Points*
	whom he can or should see. Look after him and make sure that you or the right person serves him promptly. Escort him if that seems the thing to do.
	f. Be courteous even when the other person is not. Courtesy has never lost an account.
2. Put yourself in customer's place.	a. Treat everyone who approaches you as though he were a customer.
	b. Remember he wishes to obtain information or transact business as quickly as possible.
	c. Keep customer's point of view in mind.
	d. Visualize how you would like to be treated if you were the customer and proceed accordingly.
3. Ask, "May I help you?"	a. Make it easy for customers to begin to do business.
	b. Let the customer tell his full story; don't interrupt him unless someone else should handle his transaction.
	c. Do not try to handle a transaction with which you are not familiar. Call in someone who is well informed in the particular kind of transaction.
	Many times it pleases a customer for you to go out of your way to obtain in-

Job Factors	*Key Points*
	formation that is difficult to procure.
	d. Be alert for any indication that a customer is displeased, or may be closing his account. You may be able to win back his good will and save the account if it is in danger of closing. Calling in an associate is often helpful.
4. Recognize a person waiting for attention.	a. Indicate recognition of a person waiting for attention by a nod or spoken word. Often you can draw in an associate to help you.
	b. In recognizing another person, be careful that the person you are waiting on is not offended.
5. Use customer's name.	a. Use the customer's name in conversation whenever you have an appropriate opportunity.
	b. Be sure you know his name and pronounce it correctly.
6. Look directly at the customer.	a. Make certain the customer *understands*, and satisfy him if it is possible to do so.
	b. People usually quickly signal by the expression on their faces what your next move should be.
7 Speak clearly.	a. Use short simple words spoken in a clear, modulated voice.
	b. Pause between phrases to give the customer time to

Job Factors	*Key Points*
	understand and react. Do not speak rapidly.
8. Avoid technical language.	a. Technical "shop" words mean little to customers and often cause misunderstandings. *Example*: "It will be necessary to execute this instrument, Mr. Brown, and put through a debit ticket against your account." *All that is needed is*: "If you will sign this form, we can charge your account."
9. Suggest — don't command.	a. Never tell a customer he *has* to do anything. *Example*: "You'll *have* to go to gate 4 to board your flight." *Instead*: "You can board your flight at gate 4, Mr. Jones." *Example*: "You'll *have* to endorse your check, Mr. Smith." *Instead*: "May I have your signature on this check, Mr. Smith?"
10. Avoid negative expressions.	a. Use imagination; try to fill the customer's needs. Avoid ever saying, "No." People want to hear what you *can* do for them, not what you *can't* do. b. No one likes to be told he is *wrong* about anything. *Example*: "You've come to the wrong place." Customer: "Oh, I have,

Job Factors	*Key Points*
	have I. Where's the right place?''
	Instead: "Mr. Bates at window 10 will take care of this for you, Mr. Yoder.''
11. Be alert to suggest other services. The customer may be thinking only of the service he came in to get.	a. Suggest in customer-benefit terms. *His important question*: ''What will I get out of this?'' or ''What will it do for me?'' Keep that word *benefits* before you. It's not so much what our services are but *how* they will benefit the customer.
	b. Be careful not to use ''high pressure'' tactics.
12. Go out of your way to help the customer.	a. Think of every possible way to help the customer do what he came to you to accomplish, including calling in an associate.
	b. Offer to do more. Your customer may hesitate to ask.
	c. Keep in mind that we have specialized knowledge to help customers in many ways.
	d. Through diversified products and/or relationships we can meet customer needs in ways that may surprise them.
	e. When a customer indicates he has other business to look after, see if it can be

85

Job Factors	*Key Points*
	done for him by someone in our organization.
13. Say "Thank you" cordially.	a. Show appreciation in a way that the customer knows you mean it and want his business.
	b. Introduce a new customer, or a customer for whom an unusual transaction is being handled, to other members of the organization to make him feel better acquainted and more at home. This, of course, cannot be done in all cases, so the occasions should be carefully selected.
	c. Invite him to come in again whenever it is appropriate to do so.

Master Tool #9

Five-Step Productive Selling—
Inside and Out

Visual Analysis
Operating Procedure

Standard of Performance

1. Put yourself in the customer's place.
   Offer him only the services or products which will meet his needs at competitive prices.
2. Make maximum use of your time to see people during each 24 hours.
3. Give each prospect your complete, unhurried attention.
4. Follow up each outside sale to make sure customer is completely satisfied.
5. Be alert for customer's repeat and additional business.
   Uncover new customers and new markets.

Objective: To reach and exceed my sales goal, with every sale made satisfying the customer's needs at an established profit to the company.

Job Factors	*Key Points*
1. Know your product.	a. A prospect will listen to us only when he feels we know what we are talking about.
	b. Knowledge is power. To capture power, capture the knowledge of our business, our services, our product.

Job Factors	*Key Points*
2. Know your prospect.	a. Learn all you can about him, his company, his industry before calling. b. Determine just what you can do for him to justify your call. c. Plan how you get in to see him.
3. Approach your prospect.	a. Top sales producers are quick to say, "Most of the business goes to those who go out after it." b. The law of averages always works for you, other things being equal. The more calls you make, the more sales you make. c. Surveys show that five percent of the country's salesmen get over ninety percent of the business by sticking with persistent calling, often closing the sale on the fifth call. d. The sale is often made or lost in your first words or actions. Be sure you *know* your product and your prospect. e. Concentrate on each call. Make one call at a time. As you approach him right now, he is the most important person you can know. Muster every idea which will help him solve his problems, meet his special needs.
4. Tell your story and listen.	a. Get the prospect to open up so you can learn which ser-

Job Factors	*Key Points*
	vices or products most interest him.
	b. Always use your prospect's valuable time to best advantage.
	c. Know when to stop talking and listen. Listen for clues.
5. Close the sale—then follow up.	a. Ask for the business if you expect to get it.
	b. Whatever you say or do, make it easy for the customer to buy. ("If you'll tell us on this form, we'll start things moving promptly.")
	c. Follow up to make sure your product or service fully satisfies the customer.

Master Tool #10

Answering the Telephone to Win

Visual Analysis
Operating Procedure

Standard of Performance

1. Answer promptly and identify yourself.
2. Be pleasant and courteous.
3. Listen attentively and speak clearly.
4. Get and give complete information.

Objective: Create the best possible impression through the use of the telephone.

Job Factors	*Key Points*
1. Answering your own telephone.	a. The ringing of your telephone is a signal that someone is waiting to deliver a message or make a request.
	b. To answer promptly and to identify yourself are courtesies due the caller.
	c. To attract customers and keep them, do your best to answer your phone when it first rings.
	d. Natural expression is important. No standard phrase is required in answering the phone. Some people say "John Smith" or "John Smith speaking." "Hello" does not identify. A pleasant voice is essential.
	e. Although prompt answering is a courtesy due the

Job Factors   *Key Points*

caller, equal consideration should be shown to those who call upon us in person; especially when they have made advance arrangements for a visit.

In such instances someone else should be designated to answer the phone promptly, saying, "He is in a meeting just now. May I ask him to call when he is through?"

f. To assure the best possible attention and service to the people who call us, it is very important that when away from our desks, we leave word where we can be reached if necessary, and when we expect to return.

2. Answering another person's telephone.

a. When answering another person's telephone, identify it so that the person calling will know that he has been connected with the correct phone. The following phrases are suggested. If you are familiar with the work, it may be helpful to identify yourself by saying, "Mr. ———'s phone. ——— speaking."

If you are not familiar the work, say, "Mr. ———'s phone."

b. After listening to the caller's reply, answer as follows:

If the person is expected the

Job Factors

Key Points

2. Answering another person's telephone (cont.)

same day, say, "He will be away until [time]. May I ask him to call you?"

If the person is on vacation, away on business, or out of the office, simply say, "He is not in the office today, we expect him [date]. May someone else help you?"

c. When the caller appears anxious to reach the person, volunteer to try to locate him, if that is possible, by saying, "I shall try to reach him for you," and only if the caller does not tell you his name, "Who may I say is calling?"

d. If a person is at his desk, only in special cases should someone else answer the telephone for him. For example, if the person called is in a meeting at his desk, say after the first exchange of comments, "He is in a meeting just now. May I ask him to call you when he is through?" Avoid saying, "He is in conference." "He is busy," or asking "Who is calling?"

e. When a request is received to have a person call back, always be alert to get the name of the individual, his company or department, and phone number. If the name is not understood, do

Job Factors	*Key Points*
	not be hesitant in saying, "I am sorry, would you repeat your name, please?"
	f. If the caller accepts your offer to have someone else help him, but does not give the name of a person, transfer the call to someone capable of assisting, or take the name and number of the caller and ask someone familiar with the work to call him back.
3. Transferring calls.	a. Outgoing calls made over dial phones cannot be transferred because they do not go through the switchboard.
	b. Incoming calls originating outside can be transferred. Say to the person calling, "Please hold the line. I'll have your call transferred." Signal the operator and ask her to transfer the call.
	c. A call should not be transferred more than once.
4. Periodic review.	a. Department managers will arrange for each member of the department to review the procedure on answering the telephone from time to time.

Master Tool #11

Four Tests for Effective Letters

Visual Analysis
Operating Procedure

Standard of Performance

1. Write each letter from the reader's point of view.
2. Ask yourself: Does it accomplish what the reader wants? Will he be pleased to receive it?
3. Check each letter against the "Four C's."
4. Remember it is your business card; once mailed, it cannot be called back.

Objective: Go out of your way to write the kind of letter that will cause the reader to say, "This is real service."

Job Factors–The Four C's	*Key Points*
1. Is the letter CLEAR?	a. Plan your letter by thinking out what you want to say before starting to dictate.
	b. Use the simplest words that express your thoughts.
	c. Get into your subject reasonably fast, beginning with a statement of immediate interest to the reader. Avoid reciting information given in his letter to us.
	d. Arrange your thoughts logically in the order of their importance to the reader.
	e. Confine each paragraph to a single idea.
	f. Confine each sentence to a single thought.

Job Factors–The Four C's   *Key Points*

g. Use short sentences; they are easier to read and understand.

h. Avoid technical words and terms.

2. Is the letter COMPLETE?

a. Make the first letter cover the ground.

b. If questions are asked, see that all are answered.

c. Give complete information.

d. Anticipate further questions on part of the reader.

e. Be ready to do more than is asked to accommodate the customer.

3. Is the letter CONSIDERATE?

a. Answer letters promptly.

b. Write only letters that are courteous and friendly.

c. Never assume an error on part of the customer.

d. Visualize your reader; try to put yourself in his place.

e. Write in a conversational style.

f. Eliminate all old-fashioned words and phrases.

g. Cool off before answering an irritating letter.

h. State your information from a favorable point of view; avoid negative words such as "failed," "neglected."

i. Write in terms of "you," the customer, instead of "we." The customer is not interested in what "we" want or "our" records.

4. Is the letter CORRECT?

a. Know where to get the facts.

Job Factors–The Four C's   *Key Points*

    b. Give accurate, up-to-date information; if necessary, check through outside channels.

    c. Stating facts or opinions? Make clear.

    d. Check each item. None omitted?

    e. Read all letters for correct proper names, initials, addresses, figures.

    f. Express thoughts accurately so that they will not be misinterpreted.

KEY THREE

Win People by
Communicating Four Ways

A business that has everything going for it except communications will soon have nothing going for it. You still lose if you are only able to communicate in a narrow sense. It takes four ways of communications to win people inside and outside of your business. Every one of these ways is essential to help yourself and others produce at their best.

The success of these four ways rests in turn on these conditions: management must take off the brakes; have an open-door policy that works; make these principles clear in writing and in the actions of each officer, manager and supervisor.

(1) *Take off the brakes*! Everyone, senior and junior, needs to be encouraged enthusiastically to speak up, to express ideas freely without fear of being hurt in any way. Just the reverse could result. Constructive ideas can well lead to personal advancement and increasing job satisfaction.

There are many companies much concerned about more effective communications which haven't a chance to win in this area unless they change. Their people at every level are up-tight, afraid to speak up. These businesses are run by a few men at the top who have the brakes on to a screeching point. Communications in such an environment is a laugh.

Let us say to these companies, "Take these brakes off *now* if you not only want to get started on effective communications, but start on the road to the kind of productivity, growth and profits you never before thought possible."

How Do You Take Off the Brakes and Keep Control?

Every Key and chapter in this book shows you how.

(2) *Have an open-door policy that works*. The personnel officer of Rust-Oleum Corporation, where open-door communications is highly successful, tells how they do it.

"We have a clear-cut, spelled-out written policy understood throughout the organization which states that each officer's, manager's, supervisor's door is always open—'no foolin.' Each individual is invited to come in and talk with a superior or an associate about any problem. If the person approached is tied up in a conference with someone else or is away, the individual leaves his name and the superior or associate from president on down the line *is expected* to arrange for the visit *just as soon as he is free*. This procedure is a definite operating rule and it works because it is clearly understood."

(3) *Make conditions (1) and (2) clear in written operating procedures*. In doing this, be sure you have all your operations for running your department and business in writing. Our extensive studies show that less than one out of five companies are so equipped and they are the leaders in productivity, growth, profits. See pages 56-58 on how to write up your operating procedures quickly and keep them up to date.

For your people to believe what you say about taking off the brakes and having an open-door policy that works, put these practices solidly in writing and review them periodically with managers, supervisors and each person reporting to you.

The Secret to Productive Communications

Communications is a word much overused today. Volumes are written and spoken about it.

Once you have established the basic conditions just explained, the secret to making communications effective lies in the following four-way action. Applying each one of the four ways is essential to a total result that leads to record productivity and profits for you.

These actions can be stated in four words:.

1. *Teach*—Every winning manager a teacher
2. *Speak*—Speak with influence—you can do it
3. *Interview*—"This is what I want to know"
4. *Discuss*—Use the explosive power of an interchange of ideas

The quick-reading chapters ahead will give you every tool you need for outstanding results in this crucial field.

7

Every Manager a Teacher

To keep his company competitive, growing in customers, productivity and profits, each officer, manager and supervisor needs to do a top teaching job *every business day*. This calls for communications of the highest order. Your future and that of your company depends on getting across to each individual the know-why and know-how of his job, his business, what it accomplishes for customers, and what it all means to his own advancement.

You Teach to Compete

If we are to meet our competition, every one of us must be a teacher. You can be sure your toughest competitors are using this potent weapon right now without letup. No one today, if he is to serve and influence people around him, can say, "Oh, I'm not a teacher. That is for Jim or Mary. They're born teachers." Do away with the timid thought that you must be born to teach. Successful teaching is within the reach of each of us. Teachers are not born any more than salesmen are born.

Everything you do wherever you are if you are with people, you are teaching in some measure. Whenever you are working with associates or dealing with customers, you are teaching. The key here is to make that teaching pay rich dividends. How? Make these moves.

I. Teach as an adult with adults

There is no room today in business for a teacher who uses a "schoolmarm" approach, who talks down for one moment. Every person in business is an adult and insists on being treated as an adult whether he is a recent high school graduate, has a college degree, or is a mature, experienced salesman. You are an adult talking with adults and your effectiveness as a teacher depends mightily on your winning the confidence of people you are teaching by giving them an assured feeling that you highly respect them as adults. They share together with you their adult views, ideas, observations. Build in them the confidence that they have many talents to draw upon through the learning process *because they are adults*.

"You Can't Teach Old Dogs New Tricks?"

Many studies disprove this old adage. Old dogs are being taught new tricks every day. The fact is that the more adult each one of us is, the more experience we have, the more we are equipped to learn, to grasp new ideas, to glean new information. Your experience through adult living gives you incidents, situations, lessons you have gone through to compare, contrast and relate to new ideas, new information, new incidents. Your background of such experience gives you a valuable sounding board against which to test new knowledge. The child has nothing by comparison to which he can relate and tie down the new knowledge.

You Never Stop Using Your Teaching Talents

Whatever your management position, you are using daily your ability to teach as an adult with adults. Each time you talk with a person in your group or make a report to your superior, vital teaching talents come into play.

How Young Managers Bridge the Credibility Gap

George Eban is one of a fast-growing number of young managers and supervisors across this nation who are faced with breaking in older adults transferred to new senior jobs. In this case new sales assignments were involved where new technology and the use of computerized knowledge must be taught by the young manager.

"How," asked George, "do I bridge this wide age gap and cause the older man to have confidence in my teaching? I know what I am teaching from A to Z, but I feel uncomfortable being so much younger."

"Take this two-point approach, George," replied Mark Till, executive vice president of his company, "and you'll bridge this gap quickly.

> "1. Recognize at the start that the person you are teaching has much other experience you do not have, but in this new work you have the experience that he needs to capitalize on. You have been *through* what you are teaching him. You know it. He has yet to learn it.
>
> "2. Teach him with authority and let authority ring in your voice, never egotistically nor apologetically, but *honestly,* knowing that you have the experience to pass along to him in a specialized field that can help him increase his sales production and his chances for advancement."

George Eban found that this approach won the older person's confidence completely and made this next move in his teaching highly effective.

II. Take six steps to successful teaching

Use these teaching steps (Master Tool #12, page 108) to equip each individual, senior and junior, for his best job performance at the time he tackles new work, and watch his productive output mount. Multiply the power of these steps in *group teaching* by practicing these six principles.

III. How to make your teaching outstanding

1. *Teach with contagious enthusiasm.* It takes no more energy to get ideas and knowledge across with enthusiasm that radiates, than it does to say the same words in a matter-of-fact way. Yet the difference is as day is to night. A survey among high school students puts this principle at the top of the list in effective teaching.

You may say, "I'm one of those people who by nature does not radiate enthusiasm. I just take things in stride without getting all fired up." Remember, those you are teaching are exposed most of the time to people who reflect little enthusiasm when talking or teaching. Our observations are that most people are not the enthusiastic type. This situation gives you a great advantage on which to capitalize, for you can develop this talent of being enthusiastic and practicing it where others do not. You can do it by getting your mind so filled with your subject and believing in it so completely that you cannot help being enthusiastic in teaching it. When you do that you stand out by contrast above a host of persons who in certain respects teach ably but fall far short in projecting enthusiasm.

Develop the faculty to teach with contagious enthusiasm and reap the results you are certain to get.

2. *Stand when you teach, move about, and use the board or visual charts liberally.* Your personality and your ideas register with telling effect when you are a moving picture and vary your teaching with action around the chalkboard, flip charts, or exhibits on which you visualize your points. All you need to do to be convinced of the importance of standing and moving about with plenty of action as contrasted to sitting while teaching or leading a group discussion, is to watch both methods in operation. There are many occasions in business or community activities where you can observe the striking difference between these methods.

One of the fine arts of the stage is to see that the characters keep moving as the action calls for it, often acting swiftly so that the audience is kept on their toes wondering what the next move will be. Good teaching uses the dramatic touch to convey the full impact of an idea or of a certain point. When you center your action around a board or moving chart on which you visualize the idea, you increase both the attention and absorption of the group. They "come alive" to the situation.

3. *Free yourself from notes and reading material.* Keep your eyes and your delivery on the group you are teaching. Talk with each one as if you were carrying on a conversation with them. Each time you refer to or read from notes you tend to break contact and to lose your effectiveness. The person who can teach and be almost completely independent of notes, whenever the subject permits, stands out in the eyes of the group he is teaching. It is strange that so few

teachers seem to realize what a great advantage they have here within their grasp. This ability you can readily acquire by saturating yourself with your subject.

You are seasoned and experienced in the subject you are teaching. You know your subject. That is one big reason you are teaching it. Fortified by this knowledge, simply realize that you need have no fear of forgetting to say what you have in your notes. Just keep clearly in mind the main theme you are discussing. Don't worry about following line for line what is in your notes. What difference does it make if you leave out material at the point where you have it written on your page. Ninety-nine times out of a hundred (and this is substantiated by many experiences) you will bring in the same material later on in a perfectly natural way as you speak, without even so much as a glance at your notes.

The reverse can be true if you have a habit of following your notes closely. You get tied to them and tend to forget most of what you have written. When you try to stop reading, look up and out to your audience, you then hurry back to your paper insecurely, with the feeling that you are tied to that paper.

There are two situations where the actual reading of your notes can be justified: one, where you have an array of figures that need quoting; the other, where you are actually quoting what someone said. But even in these two situations it is wise to analyze whether your teaching is actually helped by these figures or quotations. Most figures in any quantity are "dry" and the group you are teaching would much sooner have your own ideas and experiences related to them "off the cuff" than listen to quotations from people far away from the scene.

4. *Draw out wide participation of the group.* Avoid calling on individuals by name on a roll. That is deadening. If you are fully using principles 1, 2, and 3, you will inspire spontaneous participation by many members of the group. Put on the board every single idea expressed by each person and notice how fast one idea stimulates another as each one sees his own contribution on the board the moment it is spoken. This is the visual-pooling-of-ideas technique and it is highly productive.

To illustrate, suppose you are teaching the subject, "Reducing Costs in Operating a Business." You put on the chalkboard the words, "Work Flow and Scheduling." You ask, "What are your ideas for reducing costs in the flow of the work and scheduling the work? Let's have a lot of ideas here on the board fast. I will write them down as you give them. Never mind whether you think the idea is any good or not. Sometimes the best ideas spring from a thought you may hesitate a long while to mention. Come right out with it. We're going on the basis that any thought expressed may have a germ of an idea in it that is worth exploring. All right, start shooting at this board and I'll write them down.''

You find some twenty ideas coming at you from all over the room. You have trouble writing them on the board fast enough to keep up. You discuss with the group certain ideas on the board in turn: equipment, forms and reports, plant layout, controls—all related to reducing costs. Under each one you write down many ideas coming from the group until the board is covered. You discuss certain ideas under these headings.

Members of the group quickly capture them in their notebooks to develop them further in their own thinking, for here is an opportunity that does not come their way often. Each member has at his command within a few minutes of time a pool of ideas from many minds. He takes these ideas along with his own and gleans from them certain ones that can save many dollars and hours for his department. You as a teacher make that kind of result possible by drawing out wide group participation.

5. *Use many case illustrations and live demonstrations.* Teaching material needs to be punctuated many times with practical incidents and the dramatizing of actual situations. Superior teaching calls for a continuous gathering of such cases and peppering your presentation with them. Frequently call on members of your group to extemporaneously act out live demonstrations with prepared scripts and encourage them to bring out situations in their own experience to illustrate points under discussion. Keep in mind that ''all the world's a stage.''

There are two magic words that can give your teaching an electric charge. The two words are: ''For example. . . .'' You follow these words with a case illustration from your own experience or the experience of others to nail down a particular point. Very quickly you bring out another point and tie that one down with another ''for example,'' followed by another specific incident. Keep any general presentation down to a minimum. Illustrate every point you can specifically. Cases give each person in your group "meat" to put his teeth into, an idea to take away and apply on his job.

This principle has even greater value through live demonstrations. Never fear that people will be reluctant to be actors in these demonstrations, particularly if you call on a number to take parts in several scenes. It loosens up the entire group and drives home with them points in your teaching which stick.

6. *Inspire each person with confidence in himself and his capacity to tap many productive talents.* This is where teaching reaches its highest power—an opportunity unmatched in any other field.

Sitting at your feet within a business or in a classroom are individual personalities, many of whom, according to study after study, use less than one-tenth of their potential. Make no mistake about it, they are just waiting for a person in your position to touch off the spark which can open up for them new areas of achievement. Believe me, nothing happens in this world without that kind of inspirational shove. Your teaching can help vitally to give them this motivation.

Albert Schweitzer, recognized as one of the world's greatest men, receiver of the Nobel Prize in music, medicine, and philosophy, was about to be taken out of school by his mother because he had a dull mind. But a teacher got hold of Albert Schweitzer and turned him around.

Most of us are individuals just going along until this spark of understanding catches hold. The tragedy is that many people go through a business career without ever getting that *productive* spark.

Think of it. Through the three sure moves brought out in this chapter your teaching can triple the performance of each person in your group, up productivity and profits for you and your company, bring you the kind of job satisfaction you get in no other way.

Make these three profit moves NOW:

    I. Teach as an adult with adults
   II. Use six steps to successful teaching
  III. Magnetize your teaching through six principles

Master Tool #12

Six Steps to Successful Teaching

Visual Analysis
Operating Procedure

Standard of Performance
Use the six steps in teaching
so that the person learning:
1. clearly and fully understands the know-why and
   know-how of the work and
   what is expected of him.
2. desires to do the work to
   the best of his ability.
3. does the work at the
   required initial standard of
   performance.

Objective: Use effectively the six steps to successful teaching
for every type of responsibility.

Major Steps	*Key Points*
1. Explain	a. Put the person at ease —have a friendly atti-tude.
	b. Create interest and en-thusiasm for the work. Do not stress difficulties at the beginning.
	c. Using this operating proce-dure as your teaching agenda, first explain clearly the reason for the job, what it means to the business, and the customer. Always explain the "know-why."
	d. Explain exactly what the person doing the job

Major Steps	*Key Points*
	accomplishes for the customer.
	e. Explain how the work originates and where it goes.
	f. Explain the best way to do it. There is one best way to do each job.
	g. State that way positively, never negatively. Be constructive with each explanation.
	h. Simplify the complex. Make explanations simple.
	i. Visualize everything. "The eye long remembers what the ear soon forgets." Use visual analyses, chalkboard, charts, exhibits, films, opaque and transparent projections, whatever visual means will best present the subject being taught.
	j. Explain the relationship of each person's job to other activities of the business. Relationships can often be confusing unless visualized clearly and simply.
2. Demonstrate	a. Know how to do the job yourself. There is no substitute for actual performance.
	b. Show the way the work is done in sequence of doing it. Take up one point at a time.

Major Steps	*Key Points*
	c. Always give reasons. Obvious points to you may need explaining.
	d. Show easier things to do first rather than harder ones.
	e. Recognize points where mistakes might be made. Stress from your experience.
	f. Encourage person to take notes.
	g. Avoid technical language.
	h. Show others performing the job.
	i. If it is senior work involving conversations with associates and customers, ask the person learning to sit in on preliminary discussions, the actual handling of the transaction, the closing, and follow-up work.
3. Observe	a. Let the person learning perform the job while you watch him.
	b. Ask the person to tell and show you how the job is done. In effect, get a receipt for what you tell him. Correct constructively. Be quick with compliments when deserved. Continually encourage.
	c. Exercise patience. Let him do it. Avoid interfering and taking over unless absolutely necessary. This

Major Steps   *Key Points*

is the learning-by-doing
stage.

d. Show the person the progress he is making. He wants
to feel he is getting some-
where and our job in teaching is to *see* that he *does*,
as quickly and as thor-
oughly as possible.

e. As you watch him do it,
make sure he is acting
objectively, not self-con-
sciously, not self-centered-
ly.

f. Get him to relax and gain
self-confidence by en-
couraging him every
chance you have.

g. Give no impression of
standing over him.

h. Let him know that errors
are made by even the most
experienced.

4. Read

a. At this step, reading the
visual analysis operating
procedure of the job you are
teaching gives meaning.

b. Reading matter presented
to the person learning
before you have explained,
demonstrated, and watched
him do it, means little. But
now, the words lift them-
selves off the page under-
standingly.

5. Follow up

a. Follow up performance and
questions frequently. It is

Major Steps   *Key Points*

the way to make sure your
teaching has cleared away
the "blind spots" for the
individual.

b. Do not wait for the person
to ask questions—often he
will not do so. Instead,
schedule a time for you to
ask about and clear his
questions.

c. Make it easy to prompt
questions by saying, "I had
many questions when I was
learning, but I hesitated at
first to raise them. I found
though, by asking questions
that the one teaching learns
where he has not made
things clear."

d. The person learning is apt
quickly to respond, "Well,
since you put it that way,
I do have certain questions
that are bothering me, and
here they are . . ."

6. Prepare

a. Teach him other work so
he can be flexible to fit into
emergencies, into changing
needs. This gives him sta-
ture and increases his value.

b. Explain also that this flexibility enables him to utilize
his time to best advantage.

c. Equip him with knowledge
of the many services
throughout the organization
so he can see his place in
the whole picture and can
be alert to suggest these ser-

Master Tool #12 cont.

Major Steps	*Key Points*
6. Prepare (cont.)	vices or products to customers.
	d. Preparing for other responsibilities is fundamental to the individual's progress.

8

Speak with Force—
You Can Do It

Would you lay hold of the rarest productive talent in business?
Use it to move you far ahead while boosting the best interests of
your company? You can do it and much quicker than you think.

Outstanding speakers in the field of business are relatively few.
In a thirty-five year study of management people in public speaking,
conference and group leading, they rank low in performance as a
whole. Many executives who are effective when sitting down with
small groups lose that ability when called upon to talk on their feet.
Why? They are beyond their depth because they have yet to learn
how to use one of the sharpest tools in their hands for influencing
people and profits.

Here is a singular opportunity for you as a manager, supervisor,
or president, to stand out in the speaking department of your business.
The demand for this talent inside and outside your company was
never greater.

How do you develop this talent *now*? Practice each day the six
basic principles that have produced the ablest speakers in every field.
They have been tested through the white heat of more than six thousand
personal experiences (see pages 115-123). These principles work and
will work for you!

I. Speak without reading—you can do it

By this single stroke you can stand out as a speaker. It is rare
indeed to see and hear someone speak in public who does not struggle

with reading matter before him, manuscript or notes, and read or refer to this material continually. Such action can kill an otherwise good speech. So why should you subject yourself to this killing procedure?

The moment a speaker takes his eyes off his audience and ceases to talk with them in a conversational way, he begins to lose the magnetism that he most positively acquires by speaking into the eyes and faces of his audience. Persons making speeches seem to be obsessed with the feeling that they cannot talk without reading what they have to say or referring continually to notes. That is an unfounded fear. They can talk without reading if they are willing to prepare themselves and to work at it. You can do this, and the rewards in making your speaking an outstanding success are great.

An encouraging thought to keep before you on this point is that no one but yourself is aware of what you may forget and leave out of your speech. So cease to be fearful of speaking without referring to script or notes at your elbow. What you say in a conversational, informal but forceful way, looking directly into the faces of your audience, even though you may forget thereby to bring out important facts, will prove to be far more effective than your full, but stilted, dry reading of everything you intend to say.

There may be occasions where the reading of a statement of facts or figures is necessary and justified, but those occasions are rare. You can speak without reading and immensely enjoy doing it by following this second principle and the succeeding ones.

II. Write your speech word for word. Pack it with ideas your audience can apply.

There is no such thing as an extemporaneous speech. The chances are great that anyone purported to be speaking extemporaneously has carefully written and prepared the speech in advance at some time. As he speaks "extemporaneously" he may actually be quoting from his subconscious mind parts of written material from any number of prepared subjects. He is using information, stories, points that he has previously planted in his mind by preparing and memorizing well in advance of the occasion in which he uses them.

Writing out your speech word for word and then memorizing it pretty much word for word does not mean that you have to say it exactly that way when the time comes. For timing, just keep in mind the page as a whole, and that when typewritten, double spaced, it takes about two minutes to deliver.

Memorize it as much as you can, certainly. Photograph in your mind each sentence, paragraph and page on which these sentences and paragraphs come. Having done that, then don't worry about saying it word for word from memory and being concerned about what you leave out. That worry will make your speech almost as stilted as if you were reading it.

Photograph in Your Mind the Main Points

Get a sharp mental picture of the central controlling points in your written speech, then bring them out conversationally in the informal language that comes to you while you are speaking. If those words, those points do not come to you while you speak, there is absolutely no reason for getting panicky. That is the worst thing you can do. Skip it and go to the next point on the pages photographed on your memory. No one but yourself will be the wiser. Do not sacrifice the terrific advantage you have in speaking conversationally without reading, for the sake of reading an all-inclusive, perfectly written paper which freezes and completely loses your audience.

If you have, for example, exactly seven points to bring out in some part of your speech and you are fearful of forgetting one or more of these points, it is often better not to say ahead of time that you have "seven points," but to say instead, "There are certain specific points that support this subject. They are these . . ." Then if only five or six points come to your mind, no one but yourself will know the difference. Of course, it is more effective if you can limit such points to three or four, state the exact number, then memorize them thoroughly. Even then, for your own peace of mind in speaking, should you still forget one of the points, just move right along to the next thing you have to say and your audience will rarely notice the omission if you keep moving.

But you may say, "How do I memorize so I can speak confidently without reading?"

Preparing a Speech That Wins Audiences

Take five tested steps to develop your speech and to deliver it without notes.

> (1) *Write your speech in short paragraphs under brief headings, each heading containing an idea that ties into three or four main points of your speech title.*

Put this framework for your speech in outline form. Take large sheets of paper, sketch out the skeleton of your speech by starting with the main points. If these are four, put each of the four points at the top of a separate sheet. Then fill in on each sheet the headings which are your subpoints, leaving space for the text paragraphs for each heading to be written in, together with your illustrations. As you continue to build in the material under each of your four main points on each of the four sheets of paper, use the scissors and clip between the headings and subpoints so that you can expand, mount and paste the added material on added sheets that supplement the original four sheets.

Before you do that, however, condense on one sheet of paper your four points, headings or subpoints, and the illustrations. Put at the top of the page, "Introduction," and at the bottom, "Conclusion." Then take two separate sheets of paper from your pad, write "Introduction" at the top of one, "Conclusion" at the top of the other. These separate sheets you will use intermittently as you write and fill out the text material, expanding the four original sheets in building your full speech.

As your speech develops, you will be searching for illustrations to give a wallop to your introduction and a clincher to your conclusion.

How to Get Attention at the Start

For your introduction, pick a striking illustration or story which will give you a springboard from which to take off, *project* you quickly into your subject, so that your audience is with you the moment you get up to speak. You may need to live for a week or more with the question of what your illustration will be, if time allows, but try not to let a day pass without capturing it. For this story or illustration can be the "punch line" that "makes" a good part of your speech—gets you well into it—makes the writing of it far easier.

Of equal importance is the conclusion. The illustration you come forth with at the close should "wrap up" your speech into a neat package that sends your audience away on fire to act and profit from what you have told them.

When you have your speech written you come to the second step.

> (2) *Memorize it. Photographing the speech in your mind is the secret of memorizing. Underscore with red pencil each of your main points. Write the word "idea" in red and circle it with red in front of each main point.*

Be sure you have a definite idea expressed which *is* each of your main points. If you do not, throw away the main point. It ceases to be a main point if an idea is not in it.

> (3) *Underscore with blue pencil each of your headings under each main point. Write the word "idea" in blue and write it in blue in front of each heading.*

Think of each heading and the supporting paragraphs as containing the idea which each person in your audience can take away with him while saying, "There's a real idea I can use."

Such an idea will stick in your memory and his.

> (4) *Use an illustration under each heading to picture each idea. Write the word "picture" in front of the illustration.*

An idea can be remembered twice as easily if you have an illustration to go along with it. Your audience too will be far more apt to remember it.

> (5) *Now take your written speech with the markings, read it over again and again, photographing in your mind the speech as a whole, then each page, starting with page one.*

The law of association is a key to memorizing. Associate in your mind the way the headings interrelate, their ideas and illustrations as they tie to the main points, their order and physical place in the script.

Read through repeatedly each page after you have studied the speech as a whole.

"Walking" Through Your Speech Nails It Down

Now put it in your pocket, get on your feet and pace the room while speaking out loud to yourself each page as you have it photographed in your mind. Say it out loud from the beginning, without referring to the written speech. If the words do not come at particular spots, don't worry about it. Just think of the idea you want to express and say it in your own words. You will find these words are not much different from the words you had written down.

Go right through your speech from beginning to end as you walk. There will be certain spots that may be perfect blanks in your mind at first. Just skip them and go right on to your next heading that follows in your memory. Then when you have "walked" all the way through it, pull out the written speech from your pocket. Look at the pages where the blind spots appeared in your memory. Read over particular sentences which were blank in your thinking.

After you have covered these blind spots, "walk" through your speech again out loud. You will find it far easier to memorize while walking outside or pacing up and down a room than it is to stand or sit in one spot.

Build Confidence in a Short Time

These memorizing steps need not take a lot of time. You sandwich them in with your regular schedule. Even short walks on the way to an appointment can be used for this purpose.

Keep before you this reassuring thought—don't be bothered if the exact words do not come to you. As long as you get *firmly* photographed in your mind the main points, ideas and illustrations, and the order in which they come, the exact words you use to bring out those "meaty" parts of your speech are not the most important thing. You often find that the words which come to you are better than the words you had written down.

Never Worry About Forgetting

If it happens that you forget even the idea which comes next in your speech, skip it. Go right ahead to the next idea and your audience will not know the difference if you keep talking, keep moving ahead. They haven't your speech in hand.

Memory Increases Job Productivity

Memorizing through these five steps wins big for you both in public speaking and your performance on the job. Your ability to bring to mind facts, ideas, names on the spot can pay off for you in day-to-day relationships with your boss, associates and customers.

III. Use specific illustrations liberally in rapid-fire order to drive home points

When you have written and memorized your basic speech, keep it in your pocket and be alert for illustrations you can clip or note to fit into this basic speech material. Watch for them in everything you read or hear. It is surprising how many can be applied. But never twist an illustration to try to fit it in. It will fall flat. There are books available containing ammunition for use in speeches and you will glean much out of your own experience.

Where you can, use illustrations that say in effect, "This happened to me." There can be none finer. Personal testimony out of bitter experience or surprising individual circumstances can hit home on an audience with dramatizing force.

Make the gathering and use of many concrete illustrations a constant hobby with you. For audience reaction, these illustrations have far more impact than the flatness of a general statement.

IV. Speak up with a dynamic, full voice

Your voice is you, and the effectiveness of every word you speak hinges on the tone and clarity of what you say. All too many people use but a fraction of the capacity of their voice box. The result is apt to be a thin, high-pitched voice or a low, indistinct muttering. To correct it, keep your lungs filled with air by deep breathing, speak from your diaphragm, not from your throat, and open your mouth. Practice speaking this way every chance you get in the privacy of your room. Continual practice on this quality is what it takes. Get a good speech and voice book to help you. But speaking with a clear, strong, full voice will not get your message across if you talk with a dead-pan expression in a monologue, and without enthusiasm.

Practice these two points to give your voice power and conviction:

a. *Use short words and sentences.* You put punch in everything you say with this technique. You lose your audience fast with long, involved phrases. Win them with ideas delivered sharply and quickly.

b. *Avoid ever dropping your voice at end of statement.* This is a habit many poor speakers have. Avoid it like the plague. If your audience cannot "take in" easily everything you are saying, it would be far better for you not to say anything.

V. Your face, your being must radiate enthusiasm

Consider the truly outstanding speakers you see and hear. Do they not speak from the heart and soul and with deep convictions without which no genuine enthusiasm is possible? Yet how few speakers seem aware of this vital condition. A speech without this quality is a hollow one. Any audience quickly comes to the conclusion that this lack of enthusiasm means he cannot have anything really important to say, so why listen.

VI. Keep your speech within thirty minutes or less if the occasion demands

Living up to this principle can immensely heighten your popularity and effectiveness as a speaker. Someone has put it this way:

> I love a finished speaker
> I really truly do
> I don't mean one who's polished
> I just mean one who's through.

The "Toastmasters," an international better speech club, has a motto, "Get up! Speak up! Shut up and sit down!"

How many speakers have you listened to who have literally spoiled a fine speech by talking too long? Running over the allotted time, as previously emphasized, is a discourtesy which can be embarrassing to the person presiding, annoying and disturbing to speakers who follow, and can result in completely losing an otherwise friendly audience.

Many times a well-delivered twenty-minute speech will "steal the show" and on occasion a talk kept within five minutes will "bring down the house." In other situations, being too brief can have the opposite effect. A popular professional speaker commented recently just before he was due to speak, "They are paying me well to come a long distance to make this speech and they will be disappointed if I make it too short. But I will speak no longer and no less than thirty minutes. That is my practice because I know it pays. You can time me if you want to." We did and he did on the nose.

These six principles, uncovered by more than thirty-five years of intensive platform experience, are yours to use with increasing profit at a time when speaking before groups is essential for anyone in a position of leadership. They will raise your productivity on your job and with your company, move you far ahead of those who lack this crucial talent.

Master Tool #13

Use These Six Principles
to Make Your Speaking Outstanding

I. Speak without reading—you can do it.
II. Write your speech word for word.
   Pack it with ideas your audience can apply.
III. Use specific illustrations in rapid fire order to drive home points.
IV. Speak up with a dynamic, full voice.
V. Your face, your being must radiate enthusiasm.
VI. Keep your speech within thirty minutes or less if the occasion demands.

9

Explosive Power of an Interchange of Ideas

"George," began Chris Evans, Vice President of Marketing for the Beloe Corporation, in a phone conversation with George Stolls, Beloe's Vice President of Production, "I'd like to get you in a meeting together with the other department heads to iron out some important points on our marketing program for this coming fall."

"You go ahead and have your meeting, Chris," replied George, biting his words, "I can't make it. I just got out of one meeting in which I wasted a lot of valuable time, and I'm not going to make another one. Meetings! Meetings! That's all I hear around here . . ."

"But, George," broke in Chris, "We need to talk things over . . ."

"Well, talk things over without me this time, Chris," George cut back. "Send me a memorandum on your conclusions, and I'll return it promptly with my reactions. I can save a lot of time that way, and maybe you can too!"

While George's reaction to meetings was unusually strong, it does reflect the feeling of many individuals. Often these meetings involve far more people than the small huddle to which George was invited, and often this familiar cry is heard: "Do we have to attend another meeting?"

Our job, every one of us, is to transform that kind of reaction into: "Man! Was *that* a meeting. I got a gold mine of helpful ideas I can put to work tomorrow morning, and believe me, I will."

Costly Unless Handled Well

To call together a group of people into a "meeting" or a "conference" where the time and talents of each person are taken away from his own productive job, to tie him up for thirty, sixty, or ninety minutes, is a serious decision to make. "You better be sure you have accomplished something during those valuable minutes out of a production day," is the way one manager put it.

Tap Specific Productive Talents

Say twenty-five persons are taken away from their work for that length of time. That means twenty-five people times the number of minutes the meeting takes, becomes translated into total salary dollars the company loses *unless* that meeting has as its chief objective helping to triple the productive talents of each person.

Discussion Technique Is a Multiple Time-Saver

At a single stroke you get the persons you want to reach together in one place and achieve the results you are seeking instead of talking with one individual at a time. Taking them one by one you lose the value of all benefiting together from the stimulus of many ideas generated by a group of individual minds "sparked" by the explosive power of an interchange of ideas. This "explosive power," using the group discussion technique at every level of the organization, has turned companies around from money losers to profit makers.

As manager, supervisor, or president, your use of Master Tool #14, page 129, "Conducting an Effective Group Discussion," can improve work methods, save costs, increase individual productivity, accelerate earnings, win more and more customers. Many of the Master Tools in this book were created from ideas generated by this powerful group discussion method. The tool itself was brought into being through ideas produced in more than 8,000 group discussion experiences.

Sam Griswold, highly successful production supervisor of the Pelton Electronics Company, described the value of this interchange of ideas process in this way: "If you give me a dollar and I give you a dollar, we each still have just a dollar. But if you give me an idea and I give you an idea, we each have two ideas.''

Here is adult education at its best, a force in our midst as potent in its rocketry of ideas as it is in its development of our nuclear age. It is this result of an exchange of ideas between two people which, multiplied by as many ideas as there are people in a group, forms the explosive force for a dynamic group discussion.

Every person in such a group has had experiences no one else can duplicate. You are you. I can't be you or live your life and you can't be me or live my life. But we can share experiences and reap many money- and time-saving ideas that can be immeasurable in value.

Save Costs—Increase Service in Every Area

Do you have operating, management, business development or customer service problems you must solve *now*? Do you want to cut costs and simplify work procedures? Get your experienced people together, using the techniques in Master Tool #2, page 42, and in this chapter. The results can surprise you!

Involve each individual in your area of activity. Here is a sure way to tap ideas to make your and their jobs easier, more productive for their own and the company's profit and growth. Run these idea-creating discussions on company time before or after customer hours with virtually everyone participating. Keep the time within an hour or less. Meeting around a table with a chalkboard in front is an ideal setting. Put every idea suggested on that board. Have a specific agenda with problems close to the interests of the group.

Would You Lick These Problems?

In addition to the specific situations already mentioned for you to meet through the group discussion method, there are twenty-six ''people problems'' costing every company dearly which you can literally turn into ''people profits'' (see Exhibit B, page 133).

The Group Discussion Technique, coupled with the use of Key Two, ''Triple Productivity Through Know-Why Know-How Power,'' page 45, gives you every tool you need to solve these problems in your job area. When you do, you multiply talents, lower costs, step up earnings for you, your department and your company.

High Priority for Able Discussion Leaders

There is demand on all sides for this ability to lead these idea-producing group discussions at conferences, seminars, industry schools at universities, and company departmental meetings. Develop this talent and you have top management's eyes upon you both in lifting productivity in your own organization where you are and in your valuable customer and public relations outside.

Seminars—Schools from Coast to Coast

One of the most productive ways to put into play the explosive power of an interchange of ideas is through fast-growing seminars, and industry schools in cooperation with universities. This technique draws hundreds of lecturers and teachers from companies and college campuses across the country.

From our lecturing and teaching in over 2,500 such conference and school sessions, and faculty relationships with six universities, has come Master Tool #15, page 134, "Eight Principles in Effective Lecturing and Teaching." Each manager, supervisor, president and university teacher can use this Master Tool with great profit to himself and each group he leads. *You* can increasingly profit from these eight sure principles each time you lead such a workshop whether within or outside your organization.

Master Tool #14

Conducting an Effective Group Discussion

Visual Analysis
Operating Procedure

Standard of Performance

1. Keep discussion as short as practicable.
2. Encourage participation by each member.
3. Achieve specific results.
4. Follow through on points requiring further action.

Objective: To acquaint participants with new information, provide opportunity to exchange ideas, work out problems which may be presented, and obtain maximum benefit from the thinking of the group.

Major Factors	*Key Points*
1. Prepare a concise agenda and record minutes.	a. At the time of invitation, inform participants of the purpose of the meeting.
	b. Keep results desired constantly in mind.
	c. Include specific points, questions, and statements to stimulate active participation.
	d. Keep the discussion in line with the agenda.
	e. Taking minutes, summarizing points and actions brought out in discussion means capturing results on paper and following up for necessary future action.

Major Factors	*Key Points*
2. Keep within the time schedule.	a. Suggest scheduling discussions for thirty minutes at a time which will least conflict with regular day's work.
	b. Start on time.
	c. Allocate time so that each point on the agenda gets fair treatment.
	d. Keep discussion moving.
	e. Close on time.
3. Conduct discussion informally on an adult basis, using visual material where possible.	a. Seat the group informally around a table or desk with chalkboard, charts, exhibits and screen projection facilities available, as needed. "The eye long remembers what the ear soon forgets."
	b. Front row seats make it easy for each person to express himself. When chairs are arranged in series of rows, those seated in the rear tend to feel out of the discussion.
	c. Seat the discussion leader and any guest leaders around the table, keeping on common discussion ground with the group.
	d. Make it easy for all members of the group to participate.
	e. Placing on the board each idea or point expressed by a group can spark and sustain discussion. It gets ideas visually out in open.

Major Factors   *Key Points*

The contributor likes to
see his ideas there and they
quickly stimulate ideas
from others. Fill the board
with ideas without erasing
until necessary.

f. Avoid an academic,
schoolroom, talking-
down approach. Each one
is an adult, regardless of
age or position.

4. Stimulate discussion
throughout.

a. Discussion leader's role
should be as interlocutor,
after he has made a short,
clear statement of the purpose of meeting.

b. Keep discussion moving
by:
(1) stating objectives to
be reached,
(2) suitably introducing
ideas and points of
view while keeping the
agenda on track,
(3) directing discussion
in interests of all group
members.

c. Avoid having discussion
carried by one or two
individuals.

d. Keep discussion objec-
tive. Differences of opinion should be clarified and
kept from becoming per-
sonal.

e. Should there be difficulty
in getting each one to take
part, it is often helpful for
the leader to pause and

Major Factors	*Key Points*
	invite discussion of a question raised, sometimes counting silently to fifteen, if necessary, before saying anything further. It is quite likely that someone will speak up before the fifteen count is reached, and the ice is broken.
	f. If participation is still lacking, call informally on different individuals by name, asking their opinion and for ideas on the question at hand.
	g. Experience indicates it is best to avoid calling on individuals in sequence around circle, whether or not they have anything to say. Such a procedure can prove embarrassing and make succeeding discussions difficult.
5. Be enthusiastic and constructive.	a. Lead a discussion with the viewpoint that results can specifically help each person with his work and make his job easier.
	b. Keep all discussion on an encouraging, constructive plane.
	c. An enthusiastic approach is contagious.
	d. The only purpose in meeting is to get things accomplished.

Exhibit B

Do You Have Similar Problems?

Operating Problems—Getting the Work Out

Work is delayed because of confusion.
People don't "get the hang" of their jobs.
People don't understand all the changes in procedure.
Papers and work not routed properly.
Not sure what is expected—slow in getting started.
Have difficulty in getting out the work load.
Careless housekeeping; work place poorly arranged.
Desk and work places too congested.
Peaks and valleys to work output.
Lack of needed work skills.

Quality of Work

Services and performance; standards not interpreted uniformly.
Too much left to individual's assumption.
Errors not discovered until it is too late.
Invoices sent out incorrectly.
Personal differences with customer.
Inattention to customer's wants.
Work held over.
Some papers not filed properly.

Personal Problems

Leave to go to other employment.
Quit after a short time on the job.
Lack interest in the job.
Want transfers.
Think they can "make out" better on another job.
Lack desire to excel on the job.
Feel there is little chance to get ahead.
Get discouraged learning the job.

Master Tool #15

Eight Principles in Effective
Lecturing and Teaching

1. *Speak without reading*

   Reading a lecture results in almost immediate loss of student attention

2. *But prepare thoroughly in advance*

   a. Write out your lecture
   b. Photograph it in your mind
   c. Time each part to be covered
   d. Make timing flexible to allow for questions and discussion, yet covering vital material within time limits
   e. Use illustrations liberally in rapid-fire order to drive home points
   f. Tie each point to practical application in running any size company

3. *Be enthusiastic and informal in your delivery*

   a. Remember you are in the fastest kind of competition for class attention and interest
   b. To win, be alive with conviction that yours is the most important subject in business
   c. Your face, your being, your tone of voice should radiate enthusiasm throughout each session

4. *Speak with a clear, strong, full voice*

   a. Use short words and sentences
   b. Avoid ever dropping your voice at end of a statement

5. *Stand when you teach*

   a. Move about, using the board or charts in quick rotation
   b. When using slides, change them rapidly. Lengthy explanations can kill any presentation
   c. Avoid ever using dark slides or slides with small, unreadable print

6. *Free yourself from notes and reading material as completely as possible*

   a. Keep your eyes and your delivery on the audience by saturating yourself with your subject

    b. The person who can teach without being confined to notes stands out in effectiveness

7. *Draw out wide participation of group*

    a. Use many case illustrations, also live demonstrations where practical, with group members as the actors

    b. Field questions from the group by hitting each point quickly but fully

8. *Inspire each person with confidence in himself and his ability to go far in his business career*

   Send him away on fire to apply what you have taught him with profit both to himself and his company

10

"This Is What
I Want to Know"

The interview counseling technique can be your number one productive tool in communicating for profit. People, senior and junior in every area of activity, need desperately, at certain stages, critical information and counsel from their boss. Only a close person-to-person talk can bring this about. Yet it is at this crucial point that managers, supervisors, even presidents strike out. Why?

No Excuse with So Much at Stake

They are unprepared to handle this all-important conversation with individuals whose whole future and performance for the company can hinge on the interview's success. And there is no need whatever for this unpreparedness when so much is at stake and they can lay their hands on this chapter 10 so easily.

Below are typical key questions, dealing with pay alone, which came fast from individuals to their supervisors in fifteen leading companies. Can you answer each one? Can you give the kind of counsel that will cause the person concerned to go all-out on his job? *You can* do this with exciting results by using the ammunition and practicing the three principles this chapter offers.

Are You Ready to Answer?

—"Why did somebody else get more pay for the same type of job?"

—"Why do I have to do so much more to get my raise than other people do?"

—"I'm told I've reached my plateau. What does that mean?"

—"How much is my experience worth?"

—"What is everybody else getting? Explain to me how you determine who gets what?"

—"I've been here five years. Why is John Doolittle, with just one year of service, getting paid more for doing the same job?"

—"You've cut down on help, yet I have to do more work at the same pay."

—"Branches get cost of living increase. We didn't get one at headquarters."

—"I haven't missed a day, but I still don't get a raise."

Questions and Answers That Hit the Target

The following questions with their managers' replies came out of interviews in twelve other businesses which have raised production ten to twenty percent. They attribute much of this increase to their achievements with the interview program throughout their organizations.

Q. "How is my performance?"

A. Although a person has a rough idea of how he is performing, he is never sure of management's view. I tell him frankly just what his appraisal is, where he is doing well, where he is not performing well or not performing at all, and exactly what he needs to do to improve.

Q. "How do I fit into the overall company picture?"

A. Too often an individual can't see his place, or that he is achieving anything for the company. I try to answer this by showing him what contribution he has made, or where he should be contributing but isn't. I show him that what he does is essential to the end products for satisfied customers who make his job and his future.

I point out the importance of his job. If it were not important we would not have it. I must show him how his job fits into making profits for the company and a good salary with opportunities ahead for him.

Q. "What opportunities are available to me?"

A. To answer I must show him clear lines of promotion, how to develop his abilities to make his best contribution while pointing out all the benefits the company has to offer as he progresses.

Q. "How secure is my job?"

A. "As long as you produce, there will be a place on the team for you."

Q. "What is expected of me?"

A. Make sure he has an established objective and standard of performance for his job and tell him how he is measuring up, that when he meets this objective and standard or goes beyond it, he is on his way to opportunities ahead, to increased earnings, to contributing to company profits.

Q. "How can I make myself more valuable?"

A. "One of the best ways is for you to come up with ideas which could be incorporated into the business to make it run better and more efficiently."

This type of statement pulls amazing ideas and interests from people in all ranks of positions.

Q. "How am I doing on this job?"

A. I tell him specifically as I see it. I use tapes and films to enhance the individual's "know-why" and "know-how." Throughout the discussion the person should get the main interest. He is the center of any accomplishment. If the channel of communications is kept open, he really feels an important part of the team, will become enthusiastic for its betterment.

Q. "Where do I fit in?"

A. Secure the individual's understanding of his place in the entire picture: make clear what is expected of him. Provide a visual analysis of his job with information on where his work goes to and comes from, relate his activities to where he and his company add to the profit dollar.

Q. "Where will I be next year?"

A. Too often a person can't see his own progress in the organization. I try to show him what skills he has developed or that he can develop which the company will need in the future and that he will have a place.

Q. "Why did Bob Haven get the job?"

A. Honesty pays off here. Reasons must be valid and understandable.

Q. (In person-to-person interview, supervisor with his manager) "I feel I am being undercut by higher management."

A. I tell him I am very interested in his criticism. However, if I know this to be false, I constructively point out how he can assume more responsibility without interference from the top.

If you are close to your people, the chances are great that you are encountering these questions almost daily. The corresponding answers have proved highly effective in causing the individual to tackle his job with new enthusiasm. Many of these answers are tailor-made for you. Take them and use them beginning tomorrow morning.

The Top Ten

Hundreds of face-to-face individual interviews with their managers in twenty-seven other companies have uncovered these ten top questions which concern people most today.

1. "What are my chances to advance? Opportunities ahead? Pay growth?"
2. "How am I doing?"
3. "What need I do to be promoted? How can I better myself in my present job?"
4. "What is expected of me?"
5. "What is my relationship as an individual to the company? Where do I fit in on the team? Where do I stand?"
6. "Is my job and am I individually important to the company? If so, how?"
7. "Is this company I work for important, needed, responsible to the community and country?"
8. "What are the company's future plans?"
9. "What's new with the company—its business, benefits?"
10. "How does my job relate to the profit picture?"

Gain from These Studies

The three interview studies just reported, relating to fifty-four companies, deal with questions and answers of first importance to the individual concerned, to his supervisor, manager, often even to his president. How equipped are you for these conversations so that the person comes away from his interview with you, saying: "He gave me just what I wanted to know. Now, I can go all out on my job because of what it means to me"?

Practicing these three principles will do it!

I. Talk with each person in terms of common experiences you both have gone through.

One of the country's outstanding football college coaches recently put it this way: "Coaches no longer have to talk about their own experiences, because our players have had them all. We've gone through all the cycles in the games we've lost when we had them won, pulled games out when they were lost. *Together* we have learned to profit from our mistakes and our strong points, and to *win*."

Translate this principle to the interviewing process in two ways:

a. *Put yourself in his position.* Sharing together this common ground of experience, place yourself in the spot he is in, being thoroughly informed so that you can confidently answer every question.

b. *Talk with him as an adult to adult.* Throughout the conversation put him completely at ease, sharing experiences from which he learns and profits.

II. Your job as manager is to help him advance.

Two ways to accomplish this are to:

a. Give him the know-why and know-how of everything he does, what it means to the customer and his own progress.

b. Review with him the visual analysis of his job, evaluate

his performance, where he can add to the profit dollar to his own advantage and that of his company.

III. Give him every chance to bring out his ideas.

The greatest benefits of the interview technique can come from *listening* while you invite his ideas for improving the company, its products and services, its markets, its growth. If your organization has a suggestion system paying substantially for ideas accepted, encourage him to use it.

Large Bonus of Ideas to Cut Turnover

This principle leads to an avenue of the interviewing program which pays a rich dividend in cutting costly turnover. In many cases the individual, before the conversation takes place, may be thinking of quitting. The big goal is to win him back if you want to keep him. In doing so companies in these interview programs have captured his ideas to retain these valuable talents.

Here are the top twenty turnover reducers currently gleaned from such programs.

"Use the individual's talents to the fullest."

"Get him to participate and be proud of his contribution."

"Help him to understand why he is needed and is counted on."

"Recognize the individual as a member of the company, not just a payroll number."

"Fully introduce new and experienced people to department, business and job."

"Have a sound salary and wage administration policy." (Appraisals, advancement, job evaluation)

"Give recognition and emphasize the importance of his work. Get a commitment to objectives, give responsibility, convey security, both physical and mental."

"Equip each person for best job performance by using six steps to successful teaching."

"Have an effective personnel relations department working through line managers because they can stop turnover before it starts."

"Establish a complete education and training program for supervisors as well as for the individual."

"Provide and assure security for the person doing his job right."

"Make sure that each one gets fair and equal treatment and knows
it. People who are any good at all will leave a company that
discriminates."

"Develop capable managers who will treat each person well and
motivate him."

"Structure the job well; let each person know where he stands
in the organization."

"Fully indoctrinate the new worker so he knows what he is
expected to do. Follow up later and make sure he knows he
is part of the team."

"Implement good job placement practices where the needs of
the job are known and the capabilities of the individual are matched
to that job by specific education and training."

"Make them a part of the company, giving recognition of job
importance and knowing their place on the team."

"Even though salary is important, an understanding by management that other things are more important will reduce turnover."

"Each person must know that there is always a chance for promotion for those who will work for it."

"Enjoyment of his work without *undue* pressure."

Reap These Advantages Now

Through the individual face-to-face communications program you
multiply the productive abilities of your people, increase their income
and yours, open up opportunities for you and for them you could
gain in no other way. Using this channel introduces you to the power
of Key Four.

KEY FOUR

Put Each Person
Front Stage Center

"If you were left with one Key in your hand to get people to go *all-out* on their jobs, what would it be?" asked fast-moving Don Gardner of Bob Drake, his president.

"Put each individual front stage center! It is this key that has done most, as you know, Don, to raise our productivity and profits to record highs. Put each person in the spotlight with the eyes of management upon him by seeing that every manager constantly looks for deserving people to recommend for promotion to openings and to help others to win these promotions by personal counsel and specific individual education and training."

How do you as a manager generate the climate to make sure this key works? In these vital ways:

1. Center your personnel program in two major areas.
2. Make six moves to sound salary and wage administration.

The chapters ahead will give you the step-by-step actions to take to accomplish these ways.

11

Outstanding
Personnel Management
Centers in Two Areas

"Personnel development is the most important part of our business," says the chairman of the world's largest industrial empire. "Every problem we have gets back to what I call a 'people problem.' "

How can you be sure your company or department is doing a top personnel job? Just what does the effective management and development of people throughout the company mean?

Since the whole personnel function, even to top executives, is often a little understood one unless the answer to both of these questions is stated in simple terms, the finest opportunity to create profits can easily be missed. *Here is the way to make certain you do not miss it.*

You are doing a superior job with people in your company or department when you meet the "Overall Personnel Objective" stated in Master Tool #16, page 149, and perform well the specific activities in (I) Personal Relations and (II) Education and Training set forth in this Tool. Encourage those responsible for the company's total people relationship to use this tool as a daily check list and follow through.

The head of personnel administration and development has the overall responsibility, but each manager and supervisor *is* the personnel or human resources department in his area. The personnel officer coordinates, initiates, and assists in the work of those managing their departments. He continually welcomes their ideas and *together* they develop the programs visualized in Master Tool #16. In fact, the *only* way for him to be effective in the people side of his company is to counsel with and constantly work through these key people in each part of the organization. *When he meets this clear condition, success is his.*

Overall Personnel Objective

Put the interests of each person at the center of everything we do. Equip him to use his full talents as an enthusiastic member of the company, to move ahead with opportunity and responsibility to meet the needs in many specific ways of more and more customers at a profit.

Personnel Management Visualized

An adequate program of personnel administration and development embraces two major areas:

I. PERSONAL RELATIONS
    A. Employing with imagination in a competitive market
        1. Determining needs of organization
            a. Full schedule of responsibility for each person with opportunity for advancement
            b. "Back-up" talent for key positions
        2. Interviewing and testing
        3. Proper selection is important, but more important is what we do after people join the company
        4. Individual qualities for a business career
            a. Active mind and imagination
            b. Expresses himself easily
            c. Capacity to learn quickly
            d. Accepts and prepares for responsibility
            e. Personality which inspires confidence
            f. Flexibility to fit in as need arises
            g. Good sense of humor
            h. Ability to "dig" and follow through
            i. Cooperates well with others
    B. Placement, salary and wage progress
        1. Evaluation of the job
        2. Appraisal of the individual
        3. Advancement, salary and wage studies and administration
        4. Contract negotiations with union when applicable
    C. Security—physical and mental
        1. Scheduled discussions with each person concerning job, questions, problems, what's ahead

    2. Working conditions

    3. Hospitalization, illness, absence provisions

  D. Social and recreational activities

     Lunch and lounge facilities

  E. Communications and community relations

  F. Personnel policy studies, personnel research, audit

II. EDUCATION AND TRAINING

  A. Equipping each person for best job performance

    1. Adequately introduce each one to company, department and job

    2. Manual of operations prepared on each job as bible to operate by and teach by. Consists of simple word photographs, a visual analysis of operating procedure to:

      a. Establish objective and standard of performance for the job.

      b. Cut the break-in time for new people by fifty percent

      c. Increase the performance of experienced people

      d. Uncover new and improved ways to do the job

      e. Combine operating procedure and teaching program for the job into *one* brief document

      f. Eliminate lengthy procedures and manuals, and make time to keep them up to date

    3. Develop competent instruction, using six steps to successful teaching

    4. Arrange time and schedule

  B. Developing executive abilities in managing, leading, teaching

    1. Conduct the "Eight Session Management Course" with two groups as set forth and explained in Key Two in chapter 5.

    2. Six qualities make a leader (Key Five, chapter 15)

      a. Be enthusiastic, constructive at every turn and follow through

      b. Be persistent. Sticking with little things makes big things possible

      c. Develop others—be flexible

      d. Put yourself in the other person's place. Deal with the whole individual

      e. Express yourself clearly to be understood clearly

      f. Build people and profits through the supreme idea

3. Manage effectively in the three major responsibilities of a manager:
    a. Operations
    b. Education and Training
    c. Personal Relations
4. Good managing requires four functions:
    a. Objectives
    b. Plan
    c. Performance
    d. Controls
C. Winning customers in six key ways
    1. Know your products. Be alert to suggest them to many customers. Develop new products and markets
    2. Deal effectively with customers face to face
    3. Answer the telephone to win
    4. Write productive letters
    5. Handle customer's business right "behind the scenes"
    6. Work with community groups

12

Six Moves to Sound Pay Administration

Put yourself at the core of this critical arena of *pay*. Ask three questions concerning you and each person reporting to you:

(1) "Are you underpaid?"
(2) "Are you overpaid?"
(3) "Are you fairly paid?"

The crucial money game of *who gets what* turns around these questions.

If you have people who are underpaid and overpaid, while others are fairly paid—these are glaring inequities in company after company this minute—you have a must job to do. You can do it with certain success by using the moves this chapter gives you. Making these moves can change unhappy low producers into enthusiastic high producers.

Sound Pay Plan Essential with or without Controls

Whatever controls may be in effect at a particular time, any business without equitable, established "pay practices," and/or existing labor agreements, can be in trouble. To make such pay practices equitable and to stimulate each person to high productivity on his job, the six steps visualized in this chapter become priority actions. Even without any federal controls, any business operating in today's climate will find these moves geared directly to its growth and profits. Where managers have been short-sighted or dilatory in taking these steps before, they now become moves of major importance.

How Important Is Money?

A company placed this notice in its pay envelope: "Your salary is a confidential matter between you and the company and should not be discussed with anyone." A wag turned this notice on its back and wrote to the company, "I won't discuss it with anyone. I'm as much ashamed of it as you are."

The amount of money a person is paid is basic in his thoughts and greatly motivates his actions, even though studies show that financial compensation, instead of heading the list of factors which motivate most people to do their best work, ranks from fifth to seventh place on such a list.

Money Does Talk!

What factor do most people place at the very top? *Opportunity*. Opportunity for full use of their talents—opportunity to move as far as they can go.

Power in Your Hands

Opportunity opens the door wide to money and everything that money brings. And it is your ability to appraise both people and their jobs which puts power in your hands to make these opportunities happen for you and each person in your group.

How Do You Use This Power?

Before spelling out each move to sound pay administration, let us look at how you use this underlying power to open wide the door to money for you and each person reporting to you. Do three things: (1) fairly appraise each person's present performance in relation to the job expected of him; (2) evaluate his promise for future advancement in specific terms; (3) counsel with him on appraisals made of him.

In so doing you equip them to turn their liabilities into assets and make the most of every opportunity.

Each time you do these three things you multiply your own value to your company.

Success Depends on This Threefold Talent

No business can achieve real success without possessing these talents to appraise both people and positions and to help the individual profit through such appraisals. Yet many persons in management shy away from these responsibilities. They feel a lack of confidence in being able to do this evaluating.

There is absolutely no reason to have this feeling if they will apply the principles and take the steps brought out in this chapter. The ability to make an adequate appraisal of each individual reporting to you, to evaluate the job he or she performs, then bring them together in the moves shown in Master Tool #17, page 174, is an essential part of the equipment of every manager. This talent is in constant demand in business and it is readily within your reach.

Each Day We Are Appraised by Others

For us to see quickly what a crucial place the appraisal of the individual has in our careers, we need only to recognize that every day in business we ourselves are being appraised by others. We can never escape that appraisal. None of us can say, "Let me appraise myself because others can not appraise me fairly."

We are evaluated each day whether we like it or not. What others think and say about us may not be factual, but they are impressions others have of us, and these impressions weigh heavily. As long as we live, it is the impression we make on others, what others judge us to be that rules. Our whole case rests with others and the impressions we make on others whether it be fact or opinion.

His Career Is in Your Hands

The word "appraisal" is stressed instead of "rating." One rates or grades eggs or sheep, but appraises people to give full recognition to the whole individual personality, his present performance, assets and liabilities, and his promise for the future. When you appraise another person you take on a responsibility that is vital to him. For what you say about him on a permanent record can affect both his present and his future. You are in a real sense taking his business career in your hands, just as he would be taking yours in his hands if he were appraising you.

How to Appraise Effectively

To appraise anyone simply on the basis of how long he has been on a particular job is to be unfair not only to him, but to others around him. What has he or she *done* while holding down the job? This is where merit performance needs to be weighed carefully. One person may "live" a long time on a job but accomplish little, while another may have the job but a short time but accomplish much. If a person continually learns and grows with experience that is an unbeatable combination.

Make Evaluation of People and Jobs Simple but Thorough

Why have companies been without a formalized plan, or one insufficient for evaluating people and jobs in this new economic era when such a plan is so essential? Frustration is why. Organizations heretofore, faced with proposals to put in complicated, little-understood job evaluation plans, have pushed them aside to tackle other pressing operating problems they *knew* how to handle.

Pay Plans Take Top Priority

But today government actions put job evaluation, performance appraisals, wage and salary administration of first importance on management's agenda.

How do you establish a solid pay plan? One that can be readily installed and applied? How do you keep your job evaluation and people appraisals *simple and equitable*? Do it by making the six moves ahead.

1. Evaluate jobs throughout the company

The first step is the evaluating of the job to which a person is assigned. Each job is objectively analyzed, divorced from the individual on the job. Although there are several widely used plans for evaluating jobs, all are variations of the basic ranking method.

To have a common basis for comparing all jobs, the following six factors are often used in the service industries to measure the difference among the jobs (Exhibit C).

    a. Ability to organize details
    b. Supervision of others
    c. Preparation—education and training
    d. Resourcefulness
    e. Tact and agreeableness
    f. Responsibility

Each factor is characterized by degrees of numerical points used to provide a specific method of expressing values.

In analyzing each department's jobs, they are listed in order of relative importance in the eyes of its management, starting with the most junior job and continuing to the most senior. Each job is then carefully discussed to determine the extent to which each of the factors is involved. This can result in certain jobs changing their positions in relative importance. Jobs of a department are combined into "family" groups and compared with "family" groups in other departments. Like groups are then combined into one ranking of all jobs for the entire company, and job specifications are prepared for each job (Exhibit D).

Exhibit C
Analysis Form

Job Factors	0	2	4
Details to be organized—the extent to which the job requires independent organizing of "loose ends" or details of sufficient importance. Consider only those details that do not fit into any routine.	Very few details.	Jobs that are well routinized or directed but have some "loose ends."	Jobs of varied work with substantial number of details to be organized.
Supervision exercised over others. Consider number of people and type of work.	None.	Supervision of small group doing very routine work.	Supervision of small group doing some individual work.
Preparation—education and training. Include education, training and experience normally essential; also, consider length of time it takes an average person to learn the job.	H.S. education, average intelligence. No particular experience. Very little training.	Some minor special training such as typing, stenography, accounting, negotiable instruments, etc. that which may have been acquired by experience. or one month concentrated education and training with production record.	Experience in several jobs leading up to this one. or three months concentrated education and training.
Resourcefulness. Consider the extent to which the job requires independent thinking without the help of explicit instructions or precedent.	Very little.	Jobs that are well routinized but require interpretations involving a few exceptions to the rule.	Jobs requiring independent thinking and action at irregular intervals.
Tact and agreeableness. Consider the need for this in contacts with customer, public and personnel.	Jobs rarely coming in contact with others.	Ordinary rank and file jobs, contact generally only with others in same group.	Jobs having contact outside of group. May be routine customer contact.
Responsibility. Consider gains or losses that may result from this job. What might reasonably happen under present organization. Consider dual controls and other means of checking.	Jobs involving little loss or gain.	Jobs where loss would be time to correct errors, embarrassment, etc.	Jobs handling cash in small amounts; also jobs wherein errors not subject to immediate check might cause a loss to customer or business.

158

Exhibit C cont.

Job Factors	6	8	10
Details to be organized—the extent to which the job requires independent organizing of "loose ends" or details of sufficient importance. Consider only those details that do not fit into any routine.	Jobs having numerous details outside of routine and involves organizing work for others.	Jobs with many important details which constitute a big problem.	Jobs having a mass of unusual details that cannot be routinized.
Supervision exercised over others. Consider number of people and type of work.	Supervision of larger group whose work is mainly routine but includes some individual work.	Supervision over several small groups doing some routine and some individual work.	Supervision of a main division which includes some very important work, generally a manager.
Preparation—education and training. Include education, training and experience normally essential; also, consider length of time it takes an average person to learn the job.	Requires a fair knowledge of some particular field of work. or six months education and training.	Requires a knowledge of at least one field and also some experience in related jobs. or twelve months education and training.	Knowledge covering several fields not necessarily thoroughly but enough to discuss them. Requires wide experience. or eighteen months or more education and training.
Resourcefulness. Consider the extent to which the job requires independent thinking without the help of explicit instructions or precedent.	Jobs requiring independent thinking and action regularly.	Jobs requiring a lot of independent thinking such as is required of a major supervisor.	New problems to be faced constantly requiring the making of important decisions.
Tact and agreeableness. Consider the need for this in contacts with customer, public and personnel.	Jobs coming in contact with public, customers, employees, regularly on routine matters.	Jobs having major contacts with either customers, public or personnel.	Jobs for which personality and the ability to get along with people are primary qualifications.
Responsibility. Consider gains or losses that may result from this job. What might reasonably happen under present organization. Consider dual controls and other means of checking.	Work of a nature that correct and complete performance is hard to control, reliance being placed on the individual to do a thorough job.	Jobs handling large amounts of cash or negotiable securities.	Work of a commitment nature.

159

Exhibit D

Job Specification

Division _____   Date _____

Job Title _____   Job Number _____

NUMERICAL RATING

Factors	Details to Organize	Supervision of Others	Preparation and Training	Resource-fulness	Tact and Agree-ableness	Responsi-bility	TOTAL	SALARY RANGE Minimum	Maximum
Numerical Ratings									

Description of Job

ALLOCATION OF TIME

TIME   DAILY DUTIES (Those which occur regularly every day)

TIME   PERIODICAL DUTIES (Those which occur regularly at longer intervals, such as weekly or monthly)

TIME   OCCASIONAL DUTIES (Those which occur at irregular intervals)

PERFORMANCE OF DUTIES

A. *Details to Organize*

Is job routinized?

What details must be organized or handled outside of routine or explicit instructions?

Is the procedure fairly well covered in detail by bulletin or oral instructions?
If not, could it be?

B. *Supervision of Others*

Does the job require the direction of the work of others? How many?

Job titles

Does the job involve discussions, suggestions, recommendations regarding the status of others?
If so, to what extent?

Does the job regularly require the exercise of discretionary powers?
If so, to what extent?

Exhibit D cont.

What proportion of the time is spent on work of a supervisory nature? ___ %

C. *Preparation and Training*

What jobs are helpful in preparing for the duties of this one?

How long a period is required so that one could perform the duties of the job?
Normal
Minimum

What machine, if any, must be operated?

D. *Resourcefulness*

To what extent is independent thinking and acting necessary?
Give example

Does the job require the making of decisions?
How often?

Are decisions based on rules or precedent?
If so, give example

Do decisions require considerable interpretation and judgment?
If so, give example

Are they later reviewed or approved by others?
If so, by whom

Could they cause the loss of a customer?
A monetary loss?   A time loss?

Embarrassment to the company?   To a customer?
If so, to what extent?

E. *Tact and Agreeableness*

Does this job involve contact with the public (other than by correspondence)?
If so, describe

Does this job involve contact with officers?
Describe

Contact with managers or clerks of comparable positions?
Describe

Contact with other employees?
Describe

Does this job require composing letters?
Do they require considerable planning?
If so, give example

Does the job require the signing of letters?
If it does not, who does sign them?

F. *Responsibility*

What type of errors could be made? (manual or judgment)
How quickly would errors be discovered?
How much trouble would it be to make adjustments?
Would it mean a loss to the company or to a customer?
Does the job involve handling cash and in what amounts?
Paying?
Receiving?

Does the job involve handling valuable documents?
What are they?
Are they received from customers?
Noncustomers?
Divisions of the company?
Are they received free?
Against payment?
Are they delivered to customers?
Noncustomers?
Divisions of the company?
Are they delivered free?
Against payment?

Does the job involve responsibility for the care of the assets of others?
If so, to what extent?
Does the job involve responsibility for the care of the assets of the company?
If so, to what extent?
Does the job involve making commitments for the company?
If so, to what extent?

Division Manager _____Personnel Division _____
Division Officer _____Personnel Division _____

2. Secure periodic performance appraisals of each individual made independently by at least two qualified persons

Appraise each individual on each job you have evaluated.

One company has used many performance appraisal forms. At one point this company experimented with an elaborate, complex form prepared by a professional psychologist, containing 151 statements or questions to check, from which a profile of an individual was drawn. From these markings, the appraisal results were determined. This form was sent as an experiment to the manager of one of the departments asking him to appraise each department member on this form. The following telephone conversation took place.

Manager Bill Stokes: "Henry, I have your long form which I will fill out if you insist. But I can make a fair, complete appraisal of each person under my supervision 'on the back of an envelope.' "

The personnel officer, struck with the soundness of the idea, replied, "Go ahead, Bill, let's see what you come up with."

Use two basic questions. Growing out of this experience, a simple appraisal form was developed which is the one used today (Exhibit E page 164) and which asks two fundamental questions: (1) what is his performance on his present job? (2) to what extent does he give indications of future development? Three other questions relating to these basic ones follow on the form, each geared to specifically helping the individual increase substantially both his present productivity and his potential for growth.

For new and transferred persons a special form is shown in Exhibit F, page 165.

Exhibit E

INDIVIDUAL APPRAISAL

This appraisal will become an important part of the individual's record. Please give it as much care and attention as you would like from those who might be appraising you.

Name _____ Date _____
Department _____ Position _____

A. What is his performance on his present job? Please check one.

Unsatisfactory _____ Satisfactory _____ Superior _____

Please give your reasons for this appraisal, commenting on productivity, dependability, initiative, cooperation and general attitude.

B. To what extent does he give indication of future development?

Little or none _____ Moderate _____ Substantial _____

If your answer is "moderate" or "substantial" please indicate one or more jobs which you believe this person is basically qualified to perform either immediately or in the future, giving your reasons for this opinion. Does he show any signs of leadership?

C. Has a specific education and training program been completed to increase his performance or potential? _____
When? _____

D. Does he have any special personal or work problems that might affect his continual employment here? Consider such factors as health, attitude, other career plans, financial matters, attendance, and marital problems.

E. Have you talked with him about the positive aspects of his performance, how he can increase further his performance and potential if this is needed? _____ When? _____
What was his reaction?

Appraised by _____ Reviewed by _____
(Personnel Dept.)
Title _____

INDIVIDUAL APPRAISAL

New and Transferred Persons

To: _____   Date _____

_____ was assigned to your department on _____. Present Job Title _____. Please answer the following questions.

1. What is his performance considering the time spent on the new assignment?

   Unsatisfactory _____ Satisfactory _____ Superior _____

   Please give your reasons for this appraisal, commenting particularly upon productivity, dependability, initiative, cooperation, and general attitude.

2. Have you talked with him about the positive aspects of his performance? When? _____ Have you talked with him about areas in which you feel improvement is necessary? When? _____ How did he react?

3. Has a specific education and training program for this person been completed? _____ When? _____

Has he read the Operating Procedure pertaining to his job?

Does he have any problems relating to the company, management policies, the job, or personal matters? _____ If he has, have you talked with him about them? _____ What are the problems? _____

_____   _____
    (Appraiser's signature)   (Manager's signature)

Exhibit G

INDIVIDUAL APPRAISAL

This appraisal will become an important part of the individual's record. Please give it as much care and attention as you would like from those who might be appraising you.

Name _____   Date _____

Position _____

What is his performance in his present position?

Unsatisfactory _____ Satisfactory _____ Superior _____

Please comment on your appraisal, keeping in mind such factors as quality and quantity of work, ability to apply himself, new business possibilities, knowledge of his assignment, new ideas affecting expenses and earnings, leadership qualities, ability to work with others, to make decisions, to relate his own activities to the overall activities of the company.

To what extent does he give indication of future development?

Little or none _____ Moderate _____ Substantial _____

Please comment on your appraisal, keeping in mind such factors as: how his value to the company has increased during the past year, his capacity and ability for handling new situations, his willingness to assume new responsibilities, his qualities of being resourceful, creative, having vision and imagination. Include any possible indications of unsuitability for continued employment here.

Have you talked with him about his good qualities? _____
When? _____

Have you talked with him about his shortcomings? _____
When? _____

Appraisal by _____ Title _____

Reviewed by _____ Personnel Department

Tell why in simple English. In giving your appraisal in connection with each of the questions on the appraisal form, you do not merely put a check mark after superior, satisfactory, or unsatisfactory. That is too easy and can be done hastily without fully thinking the question through. You are asked to comment below briefly, in simple English, just why you have checked that particular answer. This is where the technique of writing your appraisal "on the back of an envelope" is essential to justify the fairness.

The independent appraisal of the individual by three people whenever possible, who *know* him well enough to do him justice, is of primary importance.

Appraising the executive. A special individual appraisal form (Exhibit G page 166) for managerial people deals particularly with abilities in the development of new business, new ideas affecting expenses and earnings or service, ability to work with others, to relate his own activities to the overall goals of the company, his capacity for handling new situations and new responsibilities, his qualities of being resourceful, creative, having vision and imagination.

Move three.

3. Make lines of promotion with opportunities for advancement clear

Show each person reporting to you how his job is related and contributes to more senior jobs. Let him see that the road ahead is an open one if he does outstanding work where he is, while preparing himself for advanced positions when they develop. These openings may come in his own or other departments. How does he get ready for these chances which often come suddenly?

Ned Barton, alert supervisor of the Chart-o-graph Corporation did it right on the job in these seven ways:

1. Observed his boss in his daily schedule, what he does on a typical day, who he talks with in conferences, at lunch, in phone conversations, the kinds of letters he writes, how he gets his job done in spite of interruptions.
2. Studied the problems going across his desk, the major ones, the pesky little ones.
3. Studied the kinds of people who report to him. What respon-

sibilities do they have? How often does he see them? Is
he confronted with personality conflicts?

4. Wrote his own description of his boss's job, visualized how
he would handle specific responsibilities if they were suddenly his.

5. Observed his outside civic and community activities related
to his position, how much of his time these activities took.

6. Watched his methods of relaxation to get fresh viewpoints
and apply fresh energies.

7. Studied the periodicals he read, the reports he received to
keep him up to date with the latest developments in the field.

Without warning, Ned Barton's boss took over the spot vacated
by the death of the general manager and Ned was asked to step into
his superior's place. Both moves were made quickly and smoothly
in a company that practiced each day making lines of promotion with
opportunities for advancement *clear* throughout the company.

Up Productivity? Do Away with Dead-End Jobs

See that every possible dead-end job you are charged with is
eliminated, mechanized, or restructured. In today's economy such
jobs are not for human beings with intelligent, creative, imaginative
minds.

Make this your goal: Every job you ask a person to handle has
importance, has daylight in front of it. This often calls for combining,
enlarging, restructuring, taking monotony and boredom out of jobs.
Some jobs seem impossible to change. But company after company
are changing them because we live in a new era where people produce
only when they see romance in what they are doing—what they
accomplish for customers and for their own progress and future.

Enlarge Every Routine Job Possible

Don't give up for one minute on your ability to enrich and make
more interesting jobs that are repetitive.

In banks where people are on machines sorting, listing and proving
thousands of checks amounting to millions of dollars, they are operating

these machines only half a day. The other half they work on finding differences where dollar amounts are wrongly listed or checks sorted to the wrong city and bank.

Individuals who formerly composed letters all day long for others to sign, are now also signing them with their own signatures, opening up a new area of responsibility and pay.

In the bookkeeping department, staff members combine the filing of checks with the paying of signatures, making sure that substantial amounts of money are paid to the right persons.

Job Enrichment Raises Productivity Thirty Percent

The workers of a British nylon spinning plant, through their own job study in discussion groups, tied wages to productivity in an agreement between management and the union which brought dramatic results. "This job study has opened our eyes," says the works manager. "A lot of unnecessary work was being done."

Before the study, it took 2,100 workers and 220 skilled craftsmen to run the plant. After the agreement went into effect, the actual manpower amounted to 1,664 workers and 180 craftsmen, a saving of $600,000 in wages, in spite of a new wage contract that hiked pay fourteen percent. The number of supervisors shrank from 211 to 135. But output per man has grown from 23,000 lbs. of yarn to 30,500 lbs. over the same period, and individual earnings jumped from $50 to $80 a week.

"The men came up with all the job-enlargement ideas for the wage-productivity agreement," said the shop steward. "They wanted the best possible working conditions. Management said, right, go and write job descriptions for nylon spinning with maximum points for minimum labor.

"The workers have formed small teams to operate the machines. We work out our own programs of work the day before. We look at what the previous shift has done and pick it up from there. No timetable. If everything goes well, we finish the run on one machine and go on to the next. If we feel like a tea break or lunch, we take it at the best time for us. Supervisors don't check the quality of our work. We do it ourselves and it's as good or more often better now.

"All this is just a starter. The amount of work in this plant that can still be taken over by the workers is tremendous. Control by the worker is inevitable. We are capable of running and controlling this plant. Obviously the next step for us is to have more involvement in the broader decision making.''

One Woman Assembles the Complete Product

Cutting parts from 210 to 80 is the key to one person producing an entire radio receiver. This receiver allows a doctor to be summoned from the golf course or an executive to be found in the shop. Depending on volume, two or three dozen women will assemble five to ten receivers apiece in a day at a Motorola plant. The result is a turned-on group of individuals who enjoy their work and have a great deal of pride in their product.

Individual assembly requires twenty-five percent more workers and more specific training. ''But,'' says the manager, ''the greater cost is just about offset by higher productivity, by the need for less inspection and by lower repair costs. Even more important is customer satisfaction. In some plants, higher worker satisfaction has also led to lower turnover and less absenteeism.''

These experiences in companies here and abroad show how move three in sound pay administration makes lines of promotion with opportunities for advancement clear while increasing productivity and profits for both the individual and his business.

Moves four and five need to be made together for they are closely interrelated.

4. Establish pay ranges with minimum and maximum amounts for each job

5. Compare key job descriptions and pay ranges periodically with comparable companies and industries and with going rates in the community

A. *How you determine pay ranges*. Comparative salary data is gathered and salary ranges are determined for certain ''key'' jobs. This procedure calls for these steps.

  1. To determine first what your ''key'' jobs are in a department, you pick out the jobs around which your other jobs within that department are clustered and related, those that tie into

and contribute to accomplishing the purpose of the key job. This grouping is called a "family grouping," consisting of jobs with similar related functions and complementing the key job in that family.

2. You select from the departments throughout the company the most representative and comparable key jobs, with their current salary or wage ranges, across the company structure, to compare with similar key jobs in selected other companies making comparable products and performing comparable services.

Example: In a specific comparative salary survey:

1. Thirty-eight "key" jobs with their salary ranges were selected for the survey, and
2. The comparison was made with similar jobs in five like companies in the industry in the same city, and in ten companies in other comparable industries in that city. The comparison was made by a personnel representative who visited the personnel departments of these companies and determined the salary figures which made up the salary ranges on each of the key jobs selected for this study.
3. From this study salary ranges were set for the key jobs in this specific company.
4. All jobs in the company were then grouped around the respective key jobs to which they were most comparable.
   a. The jobs were grouped on the basis of the evaluation of the job.
      (1) The number of jobs in a range was governed by the natural tendency of jobs to group themselves.
      (2) The jobs in each group were compared with the key jobs in that group (a) to determine whether the range was satisfactory for the job, and (b) to verify that the job was in the correct salary range.
   b. Similar jobs were compared in different departments to verify that the jobs were properly grouped.
   c. The jobs were studied to verify that by following normal promotion channels, promotions would lead to jobs with higher evaluations.
   d. The ranges established by this procedure were checked and agreed to by the various department managers.

In grouping the size of the increase by salary grades, the groups have been determined to provide the maximum increase to those with the highest performance, the minimum increase to those with barely satisfactory performance, and suitable steps graduated between these two extremes.

Experience has shown that the spread between the minimum and maximum of the specific job grades or ranges should be from thirty to fifty percent, depending on the job structure and number of jobs in the particular company. A larger spread tends to spill over into the next higher range and endangers sharpness in defining job values; a smaller spread makes it difficult to have several sufficiently substantial raises to encourage the individual to put forth high productive effort.

B. *How to maintain this program.*

    (1) Procedure for making changes:
        (a) Requests for changes in salary ranges usually originate in the department concerned.
            (i) The function and content of the job may have been modified.
            (ii) Occasionally certain aspects of the job need to be further clarified.
        (b) Department managers review proposed changes and new jobs with the personnel department representative.
        (c) Review job specifications. Departments should periodically review all their job specifications and notify the personnel department representative of any changes.

C. *Making pay reviews.* Pay ranges need to be reviewed and compared periodically with other companies and other industries in the community, and checked with current cost of living factors. Periodic revisions to keep them up to date are essential.

Final move.

6. Fit pay increases (pattern) to money available (budget control)

This move is all related to how many total dollars management determines can be budgeted for pay increases throughout the company in a given year. If the company has had a good year with a profit increase, and net earnings justify making more dollars available for pay increases in the framework of a more liberal pattern, this policy may be followed. If the company has not had a good year, for example, and profits are slim, then the garment must be patterned to fit the cloth in the amount of dollars budgeted for pay increases.

Management also must decide how competitive they feel they should be in their pay pattern when considering such factors as employee morale and motivation, the company's financial soundness, stockholder interests, capital needed for expansion, research and development, plant and equipment.

Individual pay increases within the policy determined are then discussed carefully with department managers and supervisors. Their recommendations on each person are of primary importance.

Today the fringe benefit package valued at an additional $2,500 a year per employee is a must competitive weapon for many companies. Coming fast as the top motivating force in this package is profit sharing.

Earnings Tripled Through Profit Sharing

A study, † "Does Profit Sharing Pay?", shows that a group of nonprofit sharing companies were able to increase their earnings per share only 118.8 percent from 1952–1969, while a comparable group of profit sharing companies increased their earnings 310.5 percent over the same period.

The study brings out that exceptionally competent management (reflected in this book's five keys) is the major success factor for companies with or without profit sharing. However, the profit-sharing companies outperformed the nonprofit-sharing group by substantial and widening percentages on a wide variety of operating ratios and growth measures.

What do these findings suggest to you as a manager? By putting the five keys to work each day, you raise your department's and your company's performance and profits with or without profit sharing. But with profit sharing you have a chance to add substantially to those earnings.

---

† Published by Profit Sharing Research Foundation, 1971, Evanston, Illinois.

Nine Conditions Bring Profit Sharing Success

Executives in profit-sharing companies say that these conditions are important to give you a top profit-sharing plan:

1. mutual confidence and respect between management and employees
2. payment of competitive wages and fringe benefits
3. recognition that profit sharing is not a substitute for competent management or sound personnel practices
4. top management support
5. coverage as broad as practicable
6. sufficiently flexible plan
7. significant sharing formula
8. appropriate profit-sharing education, communication, participation
9. competent administration and productive investment of funds

Note well that people are at the heart of the conditions that spell success for profit sharing. These conditions are a natural introduction to Key Five.

Master Tool #17

Sound Pay Administration
Through Six Moves

1. Evaluate jobs throughout the company.
2. Secure periodic performance appraisals of each individual made independently by at least two qualified persons.
3. Make lines of promotion with opportunities for advancement clear.
4. Establish pay ranges with minimum and maximum amounts for each job.
5. Compare key job descriptions and pay ranges periodically with comparable companies and industries and with going rates in the community.
6. Fit pay increases (pattern) to money available (budget control).

KEY FIVE

Multiply Your Own Productivity

Key Five is your ace to generate productivity and profits. Each time you help people raise the output on their jobs you boost your own performance and that of your group along with it. But a top stimulus to getting others to go all-out is to step up your own productive firepower. How do you do that?

There is a family cabin high in the Rocky Mountains built by this family out of the rock around them. For thirty-four years this cabin was without electricity. Then one day two wires were strung through the tall pines along which power, generated by rushing mountain streams deep below, set this cabin ablaze with light—ablaze with power.

There is a village in these mountains long without electricity whose inhabitants waited in their homes for the switch to be thrown from the new power dam. Suddenly it happened and every house in that village was bursting with light. One man was so moved by what he saw that he ran out of his house down the village street shouting "The power is on!"

You and I know that this power has been on since creation, but to capture it and turn it on means meeting certain conditions. There are managers in every business who are sitting there with this power untapped, waiting for their chance to move ahead in a big way. This will never just happen.

"The Power *is* on" *for you* to multiply your productivity in four sure ways. Turn to the four chapters ahead.

13

How to Lighten Your Management Work Load

"There just are not enough hours in the day!" is a cry sounded by an army of would-be executives from coast to coast. Yet top flight managers know this to be a defeatist's wail. Instead they have found eight practical ways to multiply the hours they have available to lighten their management load, to plug into a vast new reservoir of profit-making power for themselves.

1. Begin work at your desk an hour ahead of the regular office starting time.

Those "early-bird" refreshing minutes alone, free from interruptions and the heat of the day's battle can be the best time investment of the management day. During these valuable minutes:

   a. Do much to clear your desk of unfinished items from the day before. Get these memos, letters, papers into a special drawer or box out of sight, to be picked up early that morning and sent to persons for whom they are marked.
   b. Send on assignments to others with handwritten notes attached.
   c. List, on a note pad, persons to see or call or things to do that day.
   d. Put down ideas for projects to be initiated or pushed.
   e. Start the day with only work on your desk you need to handle yourself.

177

**2. Keep a follow-through schedule on all
pending items and check it each day.**

Check yourself on those things it is your business to follow and
get done. Check other people on your assignments to them *only* if
they have not first reported progress to you at a time agreed upon.

**3. With any stack of desk work before you,
take up one task at a time, finish it if possible before tackling something else.**

There is nothing more frustrating and energy wasting than to waver
from one problem to another. Put aside only those problems that
simply cannot be handled now because the persons you need to see
are not available, or because information or time is absolutely required
to do them. Procrastination—''putting things off''—is a deadly sin
of poor management.

**4. You are primarily a teacher and an
inspirer. To lighten the management
work load, your chief job is to prepare
and develop the people to whom you
have assigned responsibilities.**

To make this fourth way effective, each day apply the six steps
to successful teaching (Master Tool #12, page 108). Taking these
steps will assure that others are equipped to handle the load with
you. By so doing you increase both your and their management capacity.

**5. General good health, which permits sus-
tained, enthusiastic drive, is fundamental.**

For most people this requirement calls for (a) eight hours sleep
a night, (b) a balanced diet with regular eating habits, (c) temperance
in eating and drinking, (d) some physical and mental relaxation each

day (there is no better health-builder than walking two miles a day), (e) congenial family life and normal sex life, (f) strong faith in our Creator and our fellowmen, and (g) a cheerful, wholesome approach to the future.

Just spelling out this kind of program for yourself accomplishes nothing. To *do* it means following it regularly. There will be times when special circumstances find you in a jam and you just can't, for example, get the sleep for several nights which your constitution needs. Make sure then, the first night you have free, that you get to bed *early* in the evening and catch up with that sleep. You may say, "I can't get unwound and go to sleep that early." Go to bed anyway. Just lie there, and get the great advantage of relaxing between the sheets in a darkened room, and nine times out of ten you will find that sleep comes. Such experiences can be life savers for you.

Strain and tension are part of today's business world. Most of us are subject to it and we know how serious its effect can be if it gets the better of us. But this it need not do. Our job is to keep that from happening, for health and the enjoyment of living are vital to us and fundamental to carrying our work load.

One excellent, quick way to relieve nervous tension is to stretch out your arms as far as you can, then open and close your fingers and fists forty or fifty times, stretching your fingers as far out as you can before closing your fists in succession. You can literally feel the relief from tension in your nerves and body following this exercise. It can be done whenever you have the opportunity, while walking down the street, or standing, or while stretching out your legs and arms when in bed.

Is your productive energy being sapped because of your back? Authorities estimate that seventy percent of our population have back problems. As one of many who have freed themselves from this painful brake on one's ability to carry the work load at full strength, the exercises described in Exhibit H, page 180, are personally suggested. They should, of course, be done after consulting your doctor.

Another exercise for the back which has proved to be very effective is to hang by your hands from a bar high enough so that your toes do not touch the floor, counting to 100 before releasing your grip.

A report from a panel of distinguished physicians brings out some pertinent observations. The junior executive striving for the top, rather than his boss, is the most likely candidate for heart trouble. An

Exhibit H

Purpose of Exercises. The basis for proper exercises for the majority of persons with low back pain is the pelvic tilt with flattening of the lower back. The exercises also provide strengthening of back and abdominal muscles, and stretching of tight back, hip and leg muscles.

Exercises should be done on firm, hard surface in back lying position with knees flexed.†

1. *Pelvic Tilt*

    Press lower back down into floor by tightening buttocks and abdominal muscles. Tuck chin in so as to flatten back of neck against floor. *Hold this total position* for a slow count of 5. Do not hold breath. To relax, slowly release in this order: neck and shoulders, abdomen and buttocks. Do ten times.

2. *Pelvic Tilt Combined with Knee to Chest*

    Do pelvic tilt, as instructed, *to hold position*. Bend right knee to chest, grasp knee in both hands and draw knee toward chest. Tuck chin in and attempt to place forehead to knee. Hold for the count of 5. Slowly return neck and then knee to starting position. Relax as in exercise 1. Do ten times.

3. *Pelvic Tilt Combined with Both Knees to Chest*

    Do pelvic tilt *to hold position*. Bend right knee to chest as instructed in exercise 2, but just place right hand on right knee; without losing pelvic tilt bring left knee to chest; grasp knee in left hand and draw back toward shoulders. Tuck chin in and raise head attempting to place it between knees. Hold count of 5. Without losing pelvic tilt, lower one leg at a time to starting position. Relax. Do ten times.

4. *Pelvic Tilt with Straightening of Legs*

    Do pelvic tilt *to hold position*. Bend right knee to chest, grasp knee in both hands and draw firmly to chest. Slide left heel down until left leg is flattened against floor. Keep left knee straight with back of knee against floor and pull foot upward toward shin. Hold for count of 5. Slowly slide the left heel back to starting position and replace right knee. Relax. Do ten times.

5. *Pelvic Tilt with Straight Leg Raising*

    Do pelvic tilt *to hold position*. Bend right knee to chest; leading with heel, straighten leg toward ceiling. Without losing pelvic tilt, lower leg to floor and draw knee back to starting position (knee bent, foot flat). Relax. Do ten times. Repeat using left knee. Do ten times.

† Part of Home Instructions, Evanston Hospital, physical therapy department.

individual whose personality is vigorous, ambitious, aggressive, who consumes a rich diet, has sedentary habits without some wood-sawing or other outdoor exercise, and who uses alcohol and tobacco in excess, may be particularly susceptible to a heart problem.

The suggestion follows that the best antidote for nervous strain, tension and insomnia is physical fatigue from work or exercise. It is far more satisfactory than drugs for the same purpose. The dangerous age is 45 and persons gunning to be executives should form better habits in their 20's and 30's.

To lighten the management work load and get fun out of doing it while tripling your productive talents, watch these fundamentals for sound health.

6. Keep ahead of your work load by initiating and keeping several project "balls in the air" at the same time.

The law of percentages will work for you. Where one or two of your projects meet resistance or get bogged down, others will be succeeding. Always remember that "each day is a new day" with disappointments, certainly, but with encouragements as well, if you keep at it. And the rewards for such *persistency* (Key Five) are great.

Keep ahead instead of keeping up. Stay out of the rut of always trying to keep up with your work load by forcing yourself to get ahead of it. A quick way to reach this goal is to keep recommending to your superiors well-thought-out ideas and programs for improving the efficiency of the company's operations, the effectiveness of its personal relations, and the adequacy of its education and training—your *Triangle of Management* (Master Tool #3, page 48). These ideas for improvement can mean much for you and your company.

Use the two-edged sword for cost-profit ideas. There is a two-edged sword to use in cutting through fuzzy thinking to capture ideas to improve each area of the Management Triangle. In these days of the critical cost squeeze on profits, your superiors are looking for ideas that cut the cost of doing business or that help get more business for your company—the two edges of the sword. These two ways lead to profits which keep your company in business and growing.

Profits are earned in these two major ways: cutting costs without sacrificing quality, and selling more of your products or services at profitable prices. Saving costs gives you the same result as selling your product. It's a stern hard fact of bookkeeping in the average business that every dollar you save in costs is equal to twenty dollars in sales. In a typical situation a company will net roughly a $5 profit on the sale of $100 worth of goods. So if you cut your costs by $5, it's just as if you had sold $100 worth of products. The best way to increase the amount you keep—the remaining five percent—is to decrease your costs.

The forty cost-saving points (Master Tool #2, pages 42-44), will stimulate many ideas to turn into profit-making projects. These projects will keep you far ahead of your management load.

7. Develop zest to lighten your load.

Every growing business is reaching for an executive who possesses this ability. There is no ceiling on opportunity for him. The technique for developing this zest that carries such a premium is to finish off things at the beginning of the day that are not too difficult. This result, which often takes place more quickly than you thought it would while you were worrying about it, gives you that sense of accomplishment which enables you to tackle the major problems that come in the late morning or early afternoon.

Note that these two actions, (1) "develop zest," and (2) "lighten your load," feed each other. When you see a job completed, you develop a feeling of confidence and accomplishment which in turn gives you added zest for your job. This added zest helps you tackle the tougher jobs that others put off and put off.

Harlan Tilcox, manager of a large department of the National Equipment Corporation, was letting his work load get the best of him via the bogeyman, "Mr. Unfinished Business." He didn't know just why or what to do about it. Harlan's wife noticed that he didn't sleep nights. Harlan mentioned his work problem to his friend, Barry Holden, manager of a department as large as Harlan's, who consistently kept his work up to date.

"Barry," said Harlan, "I never get caught up. You seem to be right on top of your load all the time. What's your secret?"

"Let me ask you something first, Harlan," replied Barry. "Do you worry a lot about that unfinished pile on your desk?"

"I guess I do."

"I'll bet you do!" Barry was emphatic. "You never seem to enjoy your lunch, or even a good golf game like we had last Saturday.

I'd say that all you need to do to lick your problem is to *work* on these unfinished jobs, *not worry* about them.

"I used to worry about my pile too until I suddenly discovered a technique. I started early one morning to finish up one of the easier jobs, but one that I worried about simply because it was hanging there. In worrying, I even thought that it was going to be difficult. But I licked it in no time. That gave me the confidence and zest I needed, and that zest made even the harder ones coming later in the day actually seem easy. You know, Harlan, I learned that working at the job instead of worrying about it gives you that zest to go ahead and do the harder ones, and doing the harder ones adds to that zest that got you started in the first place. It's a great combination!"

"You've given me an idea, Barry. It's certainly worth a try."

It proved to be worth far more than a try. Using Barry's technique, he found to his amazement that his unfinished work list dwindled fast and with the zest which that result brought him he finished his day-to-day jobs as well. Sleep was no problem now, and he enjoyed his golf along with his job.

8. Find thirty minutes a day to read important current literature in the management field.

   a. If you have quite a walk to and from your business, try capturing some of that time by reading from a periodical as you walk (not when you're crossing streets). Some of the choicest bits of information are often garnered that way.
   b. Dedicate a few minutes each day after lunch, when you can, to keeping up with your reading before tackling your afternoon's schedule.
   c. Set aside thirty minutes before retiring to do this reading on at least two evenings a week.
   d. If you use public transportation, on two mornings a week try taking part of the time to read only the business and financial section of your regular morning paper, and use the rest of the time reading items of interest in business periodicals. On your ride back home you can catch the news of the day in an evening paper.

While capturing this thirty minutes a day to keep up with the latest in management and business literature, keep informed generally about the world around you. You can no more afford to be a narrow specialist in your reading than you can in any other area of activity. By keeping well informed beyond your own business horizons, you will do much to lighten your management load with profit-making ideas from many sources to help you and your business.

How to work effectively with others to capitalize on these ideas *now* is the subject of the next chapter.

Master Tool #18

Eight Practical Ways to Lighten Your Management Load and Jump Productivity and Income

1. Begin work at your desk an hour ahead of the regular starting time.
2. Keep a follow-through schedule on all pending items and check it each day.
3. With any stack of desk work before you, take up one task at a time, finish it if possible before tackling something else.
4. You are primarily a teacher and an inspirer. To lighten the management work load, your chief job is to prepare and develop the people to whom you have assigned responsibility.
5. General good health, which permits sustained, enthusiastic drive, is fundamental.
6. Keep ahead of your work load by initiating and keeping several project "balls in the air" at the same time.
7. Develop zest to lighten your load.
8. Find thirty minutes a day to read important current literature in the management field.

14

Work Effectively
with Others

The day of the "lone wolf" operator passed with the ox cart age, but some of these individuals are still around. There is no place today for anyone who is unable to work successfully with other people. Even the research scientist *alone* in his laboratory has gone.

World Blown into Our Laps

Four wars, a great depression, population explosions, and a nuclear-jet-motor age have so jammed us together that we can hardly stretch in any direction without hitting or stepping on somebody.

Each moment we are dependent on others for our existence. It is difficult to imagine an effective organization in any field without visualizing people working together as a team. Group thinking, not just individual thinking, is the order of the day. High productive morale in a company hinges on what groups of people in that company think and do *together*.

Working Together Is a Natural Law

This necessity of working together in groups to get things done is seen clearly in the laws of the universe. Factually, the earth is a unit. You cannot break it up and survive. You cannot take it away from the sun, from the air, from oxygen, from water, from vegetation, and live. You are dependent on each of the planet's elements and on every other part of the universe that gives life to support human beings.

People started out on this planet wrapped up in self and separated by what were to them great distances from other people. But they found out they could not survive that way. Then came the community, the province or state, the nation, then separate groups of nations. This is not theory. This is what happened. We can no more stop this movement than we can stop the earth moving around the sun. The world is a unit of human beings. In a unit—in unity—there is mighty strength.

To boost productivity and profits for each person, take this basic law of unity and put it to work through the principles this chapter brings out. Use these principles daily with both your superiors and associates and you open the flood gates to high individual effort. Let us quickly examine each one.

How to Work with Superiors

1. Reach for every chance to work with several bosses.

You have often heard it said, "You can only work for one boss." But those who accomplish the most find it essential to work for and with many bosses. The more responsibility that comes your way, the more superiors you report to.

The president of a company usually has many superiors: the chairman of the board of directors, each one of the directors, many shareholders, and, if he attains a normal goal, an ever-increasing number of customers. In effect, every member of the working force of the company is his superior, for his very job may depend on how successful he is with inspiring their confidence and in multiplying their productive talents to win profitable business through his leadership.

The person who is willing to be only a "one boss man" may find that even his one boss does not want him around, so limited does his influence become. Every person aspiring to be high in the executive councils of his company will reach for every chance to work for and with several superiors. In this way are his many talents brought to the attention of those who request part of his time and services to give them a hand with special studies and projects or "fire department" emergency calls.

"That man, Jim Brolan, certainly gets around," remarked Mark Hite, vice president in charge of sales of the Torris Corporation, to Harry Hand, vice president of industrial relations of this company.

"You know why, don't you, Mark?" replied Harry.

"No, I don't," queried Mark. "I've often wondered."

"Well, I'll tell you. When we hired him for our company-wide education and training program, he asked that at the finish of this program, instead of being assigned to a regular line job, he would like to be considered for an opening in the product engineering department as a trouble shooter working anywhere he might be needed. In that way he might better learn more about the entire business. We've had a problem filling that kind of a job, because many in the younger group feel they would be sidetracked, get lost in the shuffle by not getting into an established job in the main stream of steady promotions, where you kept on a straight path and made good.

"But that was not for Jim. He wanted to take a chance and expose himself. As a result, he's now working for three department heads on special projects and two other VP's are after him. You're one of them."

"That's right, Harry." Mark Hite now pressed his case. "We need a person badly with his background and drive to indoctrinate our sales force with a better knowledge of what our products can do, and give them ideas to use to increase sales."

That conversation took place nine years ago. Jim Brolan today has the job of executive vice president of the company.

2. Watch that your superiors are never "caught off guard" because of you.

Be quick always to keep them informed, right up to date, even ahead of date on developments with which you are working. Too often, if you are not "alive," one of your superiors may learn something from one of his associates or from his own boss affecting your activities before being alerted in advance by you. Such an occurrence can be very embarrassing to him and put you in a poor light. Contrariwise, if you are on the job and get to your boss or bosses first, they will appreciate your alertness in forearming them.

It is a matter of great pride and concern with all of us to have a reputation of being up to the minute with full information on everything going on in our particular field.

3. Be quick to give your superiors full credit for their ideas and support.

Whether their contribution is a major or a remote one, or whether it is in the way of an objection, give them full credit.

Ned Renson, manager of public relations for the American Rodendil Company, was developing with his president and departmental vice presidents a pioneer idea of producing a feature film at company expense. It was to be the romantic story of the origin and growth of the industry in which his company was engaged and its contribution to the economic and social life of America.

These senior officers had grown up with the company and were familiar with every step of its development. Ned Renson needed, as material for the script, many valuable anecdotes and points concerning the early struggles, and finally the triumphs achieved by the industry, and the future which was envisioned. But he also needed the agreement of each of these officers to spending a substantial sum of company money for this pioneer picture. Furthermore, he needed their consent that the picture be made with an educational objective and with an industry message instead of a "hard sell" advertising message huckstering the company and its products.

Each one of the officers had serious questions and certain objections to spending the company's money for such a project. If the money were to be spent they objected to spending it to produce an educational picture. They wanted a film concentrated on plugging the company, advertising it, promoting it, selling it. They wanted to get some immediate, direct return on the money expended rather than to make an educational film that promised no definite monetary return.

Ned visited with each officer individually, expressing appreciation for each idea he received to help in building the script, and for each idea as to the picture's objective and use. He patiently reviewed with them the reasons for feeling that the company would receive the best return on the capital expended if the picture were educational rather than an advertising and promotional vehicle. If the film were to be produced to educate people on what the industry and its varied products mean to the economic and social life and growth of America and of communities everywhere, there would be a wide demand for its use by high schools, colleges, civic and social clubs. In addition, their company and other companies in the industry would show the picture to their personnel to inspire them with the story of what each member of the company makes possible for customers and families by his own productive efforts. This picture would motivate them to do an even better productive job.

Ned's conversations with the president and each vice president resulted in obtaining their agreement to produce the picture with the objectives he presented. He gave each one full credit not only for their ideas for the script material but for having a major part in launching the film idea itself. The picture proved an outstanding success and they were proud to be identified with it.

4. Seek every chance to get your superiors' ideas and views.

Not to seek out your superiors' views is one sure way to lose their cooperation and much of your own effectiveness.

Frank Stirdell, manager of personnel and development for the Marleen Corporation, had twenty-two persons holding executive positions senior to his with whom he consulted regularly concerning changes in personnel policy or new personnel programs affecting people working in their areas of responsibility. Technically he reported to Marvin Verd, vice president in charge of personnel and development, but both men had learned through much experience that policy changes and new programs were put through smoothly only when each one of these executives was given an opportunity *in advance* to express his ideas and views.

Furthermore, these ideas often caused valuable revisions in personnel programs which made Frank's and Marvin's jobs easier because the result was a more popular acceptance of these programs throughout the organization.

5. Be prompt and concise in reporting on your work done and progress made.

Make your reports brief and to the point and not too frequently or too far between. Judgment enters in here to save time and to get things done with dispatch. If you study your superior's own actions in this area with persons to whom *he* reports, you are likely to find him making full use of this principle. Also you are likely to observe his particular habit of promptness and frequency of reports which can give you a cue in *your* dealings with him.

Generally, a superior should be contacted only when it seems necessary and then on questions or problems on which facts have been concisely assembled. If it is a matter that can be settled quickly, often much time can be saved by telephoning instead of trying to see him personally. Always keep before you the key thought that every contact you make should help meet his problems, his opportunities.

How to Work with Associates

To work effectively with everyone who is *not* your superior is even more important. Unless you win them, any business you have with your boss ceases to be. You are where you are because of the respect you win from those working with you, including your fellow executives. How do you win and keep winning that respect so necessary to your own progress? Your use of these four principles will take you to this goal.

1. Be quick to give them all the credit for everything you accomplish with them. Take no credit yourself.

Never fear that proper credit will not come to you in due course from the person to whom you report. When he and others above you see what boosters you have in those with whom you work, largely because you are continually giving them the credit, your superiors will be quick to see that you are building others. A top performer always strives for this kind of result.

2. Always be quick to congratulate your associates on achievements and promotions. Take every occasion to help them to these ends.

Never be jealous of their progress. It can only make you miserable and throttle your power to progress yourself. Continue to give them credit by telling other people in the organization. In this way you generate boosters for you, your ideas and projects at some time in the future when you may be needing their support. Their friendship *then* proves to be just the extra push to put over such projects.

3. Be alert to return a boost or favor given you by an associate.

This principle is important even when such situations as overtime or conflicts in vacation time are involved. "Giving" or "trading" when you can, without hurting anyone, is the essence of working together cooperatively. It is extremely important when it involves some major project on which an associate is having difficulty.

Dick Sammons, the sales manager of Danforth Corporation, was complaining at lunch one day of the big sale that he was about to lose. Ed Lavater, Danforth's comptroller, listened sympathetically and volunteered to prepare some special comparison charts that might assist Dick in his sales presentation. Ed spent many extra hours preparing the charts for Dick. The charts were the clinching factor in Dick's making the sale.

Dick never forgot the unselfish and generous way in which Ed had helped him out. The time came when Ed was trying to get a new accounting system accepted by the Board of Directors and was having trouble getting his ideas across. Now it was Dick's time to return the favor and he jumped in with all of the sales skill and experience at his command. He helped Ed work up a presentation that got enthusiastic approval from the Board. The alertness of each man to give an assist to the other was the determining factor in two successes.

4. Keep your associates well informed on things that concern them and in which you have a distinct responsibility.

People are afraid of what they do not know. This fear is particularly evident in connection with company programs dealing with such projects as broad installation of automation, mechanization, computerizing, changes in pension plan provisions, and the setting up or changing of a profit-sharing plan.

The director of personnel and consumer relations, Havelock Payloft, was well aware that rumors of these contemplated changes were particularly disturbing to senior members of the company, with long periods of service, who had much at stake. He knew also that managers of departments to whom these senior members might be directing anxious questions had not yet had opportunity to be brought up to date with current plans, since the small internal groups charged with the study and development of these programs had only recently made their recommendations to the president and board of directors.

The decision to accept the recommendations to go ahead with the automation program and to study further the provisions for changing the pension and profit-sharing plans had been made only the day before. Payloft had just come from a briefing session in the president's office.

Acting on this principle 4, "Keep your associates well informed on things that concern them," he had arranged immediately with the president to get the true story of these current developments promptly throughout the organization. He called the department managers together and that same day they started to tell this story in each department with opportunity for questions. Department members were told when and where the new machines would be installed, what jobs would be affected, that no person would lose employment because of these changes. Each person on the job where machines would be used would be given adequate education and training for other work where advancement was possible as opportunity developed. The long-term cost savings that would result from these machine installations were outlined with their projected effect on company profits. The studies for liberalizing the company's pension and profit-sharing plans were mentioned as being in process and that any possible changes would be safeguarded, and could be particularly beneficial to a person with a substantial period of service.

These information sessions were warmly received throughout the company. They completely set at rest the false rumors that had been circulating, and lifted the morale of the entire organization.

Your use of this fourth principle can be one of your strongest assets in working effectively with associates.

Team Action to Meet Deadlines

Often your ability to work constructively with others is put under the most severe test when doing a group job by a deadline date. Today these "under-the-gun assignments" are happening not only within organizations but to quickly bring companies together, small and large. As manager, supervisor, or president such an experience could hit suddenly out of the blue.

Are You Ready for It?

You will be ready for it if you use the principles brought out in this chapter and the qualities that make a leader in the chapter ahead.

Sandy Whitson drew on every one of these life savers the other day in a merger of his company, the Farsite Corporation, with another, the Parke Seldon Company. Sandy headed a production department of 150 people and the personnel of the corresponding production department of the Parke Seldon organization numbered 65.

The contemplated merger of the two companies had been pending for several weeks and there was no certainty that it would be voted through by the directors and stockholders of Parke Seldon. Wayne Seldon, chairman of the board, and majority stockholder, although he could see some decided monetary advantages to the merger, did not like being overshadowed and dominated by the Farsite Corporation, should the merger take place. He had yet to reach his decision. Due to certain competitive marketing advantages, the merger should be effective within two months. It was now December 15th.

Sandy Whitson's problem, together with the managers of the other departments of his company, was this: he was told on December

15th that he should be ready on one month's notice to take over into his department all of the people and the equipment from the corresponding production department of Parke Seldon. He must be prepared to fit each person fairly into his organization, producing effectively on his job and working cooperatively with other members of the combined departments so that production schedules would be maintained without serious interruption. Assurance would be given by the heads of both companies that no person would be released because of the merger.

Following his participation in preplanning conferences with other department managers, Sandy, seeing that full consideration and suitable placement of individual people was his biggest problem, took these steps:

1. With his supervisors and their counterparts in Parke Seldon, he discussed each person in Parke Seldon's production department, their qualifications, salary or wage, and their job.
2. Arranged to chart what each individual's new job would be and location, what tools and equipment he would need, who would be his boss, what changes and requirements in space would be needed.
3. Figured how the cost of these additional people, the space and equipment required, would fit into his departmental budget, and what larger budget total he would need to recommend, taking into account the normal turnover in personnel and letting that turnover run off without replacement.
4. Set up education and training group and individual discussions to introduce each person to his new combined company, new associates, new job, new procedures, new work environment.
5. Arranged to make sure a sufficient number of qualified people would be working in the department over the weekend to get set to accomplish the merger so that the transition would move smoothly and the regular production flow would be maintained.

As it turned out, Wayne Seldon decided he would go along with merger plans. Stockholder and other necessary approvals then followed. The announcement was made on January 15th that the physical merger would take place on Monday, February 12th. Sandy Whitson and the other department heads were ready. The merger was accomplished with a minimum of disturbance. They had won the vital cooperation of many individuals, superiors and associates to achieve an exciting goal under pressure against a deadline.

Each manager cited in this chapter got his results and multiplied his own productivity by using the principles of working effectively with others. But each one possessed something far greater. Turn to chapter 15.

Master Tool #19

For High Productivity
Work Effectively with Others

How to Work with Superiors

1. Reach for every chance to work with several bosses.
2. Watch that your superiors are never "caught off guard" because of you.
3. Be quick to give your superiors full credit for their ideas and support.
4. Seek every chance to get your superiors' ideas and views.
5. Be prompt and concise in reporting on your work done and progress made.

How to Work with Associates

1. Be quick to give them all the credit for everything you accomplish with them. Take no credit yourself.
2. Always be quick to congratulate your associates on achievements and promotions. Take every occasion to help them to these ends.
3. Be alert to return a boost or favor given you by an associate.
4. Keep your associates well informed on things that concern them and in which you have a distinct responsibility.

15

What Makes a Leader

"Why do executives die young?" asked a concerned fast-working president who sees this growing trend throughout industry.

He got this answer: "Because too many try to be a one-man band instead of conductors of an orchestra. You're like a football coach. He can't run out on the field and do the playing himself. He must do that playing through eleven other men on the field." This takes leadership of the highest order.

"What qualities make a leader?" We have thrown this question into the cross fire of group discussions participated in by more than 15,000 managers from coast to coast. Out of the white heat of these experience-packed huddles have come these six game-winning attributes.

1. Be enthusiastic, constructive at every turn and follow through

No one likes a sour puss. Each hour our job is to live the philosophy of the new day. Today may be black with problems, disappointments, headaches, the worst day you have ever seen. Everything goes wrong. "How did I ever get into this business, anyway?" you ask yourself. But reflect that feeling for one moment to those around you and you are through as a leader. Always believe that tomorrow is a new day, a day with a rainbow. Never lose that philosophy if you want to win people. Remember, it is always darkest before the dawn.

An enthusiastic, constructive approach is as refreshing as it is rare, as rare as the smile that goes with it. Look around you as you go through the day in the office or plant, on the bus, or in the wheeling and dealing in the market place. How many people do you see smiling? You see a lot of other expressions so when you smile you stand out like a diamond by contrast. I don't mean smiling like a cheshire cat. A genuine smile will always identify you, and an enthusiastic, constructive approach will draw people to you like a magnet.

President Woodrow Wilson once said of himself:

> As a beauty I am not a great star
> There are others more handsome, by far,
> But my face—I don't mind it
> For I am behind it—
> It's the people in front get the jar!*

If some of us must jar people with our faces, let's jar them pleasantly with a genuine smile. When you do that, you will never be like the man who spent $5,000 to get rid of bad breath and then discovered people didn't like him anyway.

When you have that enthusiastic approach and actually *live it*, you make a point to compliment at least three people each day for something they have done. You may say, "How can I find three people a day to congratulate?" Let us suggest they are all around us, many of them our own associates, or customers, or members of our own family. It may be a little thing but it's something that counts in their life and they are proud of it. Too often it goes by without any compliment whatever coming their way.

People are hungry for rightful praise. It can turn night into day for them. You make it all possible by a little planned thoughtfulness. Think what it does to give them an enthusiastic approach toward living—a tremendous charge in what they are doing. With that action on your part you charge your own productive batteries as surely as anything you will ever do.

Follow-through Must Be Complete

It's not enough just to smile and be enthusiastic. The constructive one-two punch must be operating.

---

* From Anthony Euwer, "My Face," *An Anthology of American Verse,* Oscar Williams (ed.), (New York, 1966), by permission of The World Publishing Company.

Larry Brown, supervisor, came to his manager, Cliff Martin, with this question: "Cliff, I know we can up the production of my group by twenty percent if we can change the flow of work layout that gears into Prent Clow's department, but Prent doesn't see it that way. Would you help?"

Larry's manager was tempted to answer, "Try again with Prent, Larry. I'm up to my ears with my own problems right now." But he caught himself, realized that helping both Larry and Prent is one of the big reasons he is getting a manager's pay.

"Sure, Larry," he replied, "I'm working on a ticklish problem myself, but that can wait. Let's get together with Prent and figure out a plan that will lift production for you both."

Here is leadership that scores. But the follow-through must be complete. If the manager tells Larry he will need to do some checking on his problem before he can sit down with him and Prent, and then gets busy with something else, forgetting to check, his leadership influence with Larry becomes minus zero.

People in every company desperately want the encouragement and backing which an enthusiastic follow-through gives them. It is often all that is needed to make them top producers.

2. Be persistent. Sticking with little things makes big things possible.

Every big accomplishment starts with a small beginning.

Not far from our mountain cabin you take but a few steps between the beginnings of two tiny streams on top of the Great Continental Divide, each stream producing a mighty river system for America, one flowing to the Atlantic Ocean, the other to the Pacific. A short hike from this spot, the fabulous Colorado River starts from tiny trickles in mountaintop snows which becomes in the valley below a herculean force, turning power stations which run gigantic industrial machines throughout that vast southwest area.

Little kernels of ideas in the minds of managers, supervisors and presidents lead to ideas big enough to give new life and growth to their companies. Seed thinking often creates new products, major cost reductions, a money-making sales pitch, a specific profit-sharing plan that lifts the morale and productivity of the whole organization.

Large Cost Savings Come from Small Items

Managers who are leaders practice this quality of sticking with little things to make big things possible by projecting their thinking to the individual on the job.

An aircraft company mechanic noted that clip nuts used to hold floor panels to Boeing airplane structures were similar to small standard clip nuts obtainable in any industrial hardware store. The Boeing nuts cost $3.10 each but the commercial ones 12 cents. When the mechanic led a Federal Administration investigation resulting in approval to substitute the 12 cent nuts, his company saved a recurring $25,479 a year on this item alone. This saving is just one of many totaling $800,000 in a year through the company's employee idea program, part of a worldwide effort to cut wasteful practices, purchases and procedures.

These efforts are being repeated all through industry. Economic belt-tightening has caused management to take hard looks at all costs of "in-house" operations with the intent to save dollar wasters which increase production costs. All of these programs lead to wider "employee involvement," higher employee morale and increased production as well as savings. Many companies have arrangements for sharing savings with the idea men through bonus payments. Other companies use the incentive of "upgrading each contributor toward earlier promotion in job or grade." †

Dale Sears, head of a highly motivated profit-making company, uses two principles to make big things possible out of small beginnings.

1. Never consider any idea too small if you can see it as a tool to accomplish a larger result. For example, it may at the moment solve only a small, local situation. But don't stop there. Be persistent. Look at all angles. See if there is a chance of the little thing you worked out applying to other departments, to changing any part of a method or system that is company wide.
2. Even if the little job is just a task to be done, do it completely, wrap it up, deliver it with no loose ends. One loose string may let a whole package break loose, cause big leaks in profit dollars.

---

† Wayne Thornis, Aviation Editor, Chicago Tribune Press Service.

The plain fact is that "loose ends" in any business can drive you crazy. Investment securities dealers have found out that they can paralyze you.

3. Develop others—be flexible

This quality is a master key to leadership. Developing others takes into account the whole know-why, know-how education and training process with each person reporting to you (Key Two).

Phil Dart, general manager for the Universal Service Corporation, recently walked through every department of his company, observing the tops of managers' and supervisors' desks. "I was shocked by what I saw," he said. "Out of 300 desks there were just five that were not loaded with papers and files. Suddenly those desk tops dramatized for me where a big chunk of our company's profits was going."

He called his entire management group together. They decided to make a film on the job of managing. They wrote their own script. They helped pick the professional actors, and it was professionally produced. But it was their product born out of the problem of freeing key officers, managers and supervisors from a multitude of details covering their desks so that they have time to manage, time to teach, time to multiply themselves through others.

A key scene in this picture which brought requests to show the film in hundreds of companies from coast to coast and in twelve countries abroad (though they made it just to improve their own managing) was this idea:

Supervisor Ray to Manager Ed: "Sure, I ought to be developing people, getting my job done through others, but when am I going to find the time? Look at my desk! I can't get out from under that pile."

In a flash this film gave the answer through manager Ed: "Ray, you never will *just find* the time. The only way to capture that time and multiply it is to take time by the forelock *now*. Don't let that pile of other people's work on your desk get one item bigger. Dispose of it now by throwing the ball to those around you. Give them the chance to catch it and run with it. But be sure you teach them what to do with that ball when they catch it."

High Premium on Flexibility

Multiplying your time through those around you springs you free from your desk, makes you flexible, able to adjust quickly to changes. That person who can fit quickly into the changing needs of his company and of customers is constantly sought out. Have more than one string to your bow.

The tragedy of being rigid, frozen in his own tracks is seen in this recent conversation about their boss, Tom, between Harry and Bob at adjoining desks.

> *Harry*: Bob, I'm in a spot with a customer. Tom has always thought he had to handle this business himself, and now he's on vacation and I've got to act without him. The customer wants action and I need a lot of information Tom is carrying around in his head on a fishing trip in Minnesota.
>
> *Bob*: You think you've got troubles. You know that Golden Blue Label business that Tom has been handling? Well, they just raked me over the coals because I didn't know the answer. Now I'm really sunk because my answer is on the same fishing trip with yours.

Unknown to this boss, his name is being considered with others for a job with greater responsibilities. Do you think he will get it? Here is the case of a ''lone operator'' on vacation with all information.

Be Flexible to Be Productive

We have asked the following question of hundreds of management groups over a thirty-year span: ''Who of you in this room is in the kind of business you planned for when you first got out of school?'' Those who say ''yes'' to that question account for less than three percent of each group. What does this result tell us? It is striking evidence of the flexibility of successful managers, ninety-seven percent of whom have adjusted their whole career to fields they had no idea they would be engaged in when they completed their academic schedule.

Teach flexibility to each person around you. Give them and you
this sharp tool to produce and go far as a leader in a fast-changing
economy.

4. Put yourself in the other person's place.
Deal with the whole individual.

When you do that you put to work more of the qualities of a leader
than you will find in any other single act. Here is a manager who
is criticizing John Wade for a mistake he made on his job which
hurt customer business. He asks John, "How could you *do it?*"

By that single question and the tone with which it was asked, he
did anything but put himself in the other person's place. Look for
a moment at Figure 1. All he could think of was John and a job.
But John and his job is only one part of this dynamic circle of life
which makes up John's total individual personality, see Figure 2.

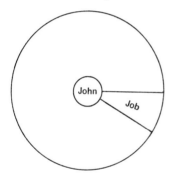

Figure 1

Figure 2

John has a family relationship in this circle. If the manager had
put himself in John's place, he may have found that John was up
the night before with a wife or child who was seriously ill, and this
experience had a definite influence in causing the mistake. John may
have a health problem himself, or a financial problem. John's background, education, experience, religious faith, ideals, social and politi-
cal viewpoints, his philosophy of life, all may have a bearing at times
on his actions. They all go to make up his total individual personality,
different in many respects from that of any other person, yet his hopes,
aspirations, frustrations, and desires are even as yours and mine. Unless

John's manager actually tries to put himself in John's place in this situation, his effectiveness as a leader is little short of zero.

Deal with the Whole Individual

Putting yourself in the other person's place calls for becoming sensitive to the four sides of his being (Figure 3). How he develops these four sides may influence everything he does, how he performs on his job and away from it. Such development can help him keep his balance in contending with environmental problems: getting to and from work, congested surroundings, pollution, drugs, crime, housing, health and living costs, raising a family, and educating his children. The moment one becomes lopsided, through neglect or overemphasis on any of these sides, at that moment we slip in our relationships with our family, friends, associates, employer, our customers, and with everyone whose esteem we prize. To get out of balance physically, intellectually, socially or spiritually is to invite trouble at every turn.

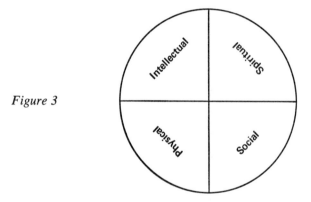

Figure 3

The fine truth is that the person who would make the most of each talent he possesses is not the narrow one- or two-sided specialist or technical genius. He is the fully rounded person with depth, breadth, imagination and vision in all four areas.

How do you help both yourself and the other person to produce at your best on the job and away from it, by developing these four sides in balance? Use, and when appropriate suggest to others, this four-step formula.

1. *Physical*   Stay competitive, maintain energy and drive through sound health (Chapter 13 page 177).

2. *Intellectual*   Be equipped with the complete know-why, know-how of your job, your business, what you accomplish for customers by your efforts (Key Two, page 45).

3. *Social*   Work cooperatively with others to achieve your best personal relations, job relations, customer and community relations (Chapter 14, page 185, also Key Three, page 97).

4. *Spiritual*   Develop high morale, an enthusiastic attitude toward your employer, customers, associates, family, friends, having strong faith in a Creator (Key One, page 19 and Key Five, page 175).

In addition to the specific Key and chapter references cited above, each Key and chapter of this book offers other ways to bring out the productive talents of the whole person.

The fifth quality that makes a leader.

5. Express yourself clearly to be understood clearly

How often has a key person talked with an individual and when he has finished, the individual says to a buddy, "I wonder what that guy was talking about." He failed to make things clear by the clear use of simple words. Key Three, "Communicate Four Ways to Profits," gives this quality a high place in the arsenal of a productive manager. Our purpose here is to pinpoint how vital it is for every manager, supervisor, or president each day to speak clearly and simply, with the other person's interest foremost in mind.

How a manager handles individual conversations determines in a major way his capacity to be a leader. Practice these four techniques to make sure you talk with a person so as to be clearly understood: (1) use simple words; (2) speak to the point but be gracious and helpful; (3) take responsibility for what you tell people; (4) if a go-between is necessary, rehearse just how the message should be said. If you are wondering whether your conversations are all being clearly understood, check yourself on these four points and watch the clarity of what you tell people improve.

A capable manager—a leader—needs to express himself clearly in all individual wage and salary questions. The use of techniques (1) and (2) left much to be desired in the following situation.

This manager is having a rough time trying to convey to Miss Tarry that her current performance does not justify a raise for her at this particular time. He has been negligent in not clearly correcting her long before.

> Manager: Miss Tarry, I wish your work were of such a nature that it warranted more consideration compensatory-wise than it indicates. It is good at times, but at other times it does not measure up to the extent of an inclusion in this present salary study.
>
> Miss Tarry: Listen, Mr. Rambly, I don't know what you are mumbling about, but if you are trying to tell me I don't get a raise, I want to know why in simple one-syllable words. This is the first inkling I've had that my work wasn't all right. It must be or you certainly would have told me long before this just where I'm not meeting your standards. Or did you mean to tell me I'm getting a raise and how much will it be?

Take responsibility for what you tell people. The next situation shows how not observing this technique (3) played havoc with the respect which every manager who is a real leader needs to have from those reporting to him.

"But Mr. Harwin," commented George James to his manager, "I understood from you that my chance of getting a raise this year was very good, and now you say I do not get one."

"I'm sorry, George," replied Harwin, "I recommended you to the Personnel Department for a raise, but I can't get it through. They told me it just was not in the cards this year, so there is nothing we can do about it."

How much respect will George have for his manager after that conversation and how far will this manager get in motivating George to produce at his best? The manager and supervisor should be the Personnel or Industrial Relations Department where they are. When a manager talks with a member of his own group, it should be the management of the company speaking.

The importance of properly using technique (4), "If a go-between is necessary, rehearse just how the message should be said," is shown in the following incident. Unless what the conveyor of the message is to say is made clear to her, the recipient may feel the lines of authority are being reversed on him.

"Will you tell Mr. Brown," said Mr. Jones, the manager to his secretary, Miss Henley, "that I hope he will be able to make the changes he spoke about by Thursday, if possible."

"Will you please arrange to make the changes Mr. Jones spoke with you about by Thursday," said Miss Henley to Mr. Brown.

"Since when was Miss Henley made my superior?" thought Mr. Brown to himself. "Why doesn't Mr. Jones tell me himself what he wants?"

If, for some urgent reason, which should be very exceptional, the manager needs to relay some information through an assistant, how much better it could sound if he had coached Miss Henley so that she said something like this: "Mr. Jones wonders, do you think in your judgment you will be able to make the changes you and he spoke about by Thursday?"

What we say and how we say it can spell the difference between a high producer and a poor one. Continuous use of the four techniques in individual conversations can insure your speaking effectively and being understood clearly on each occasion. It becomes the hallmark of a solid leader.

Avoid ever discounting the high cost in productivity that can result from these crucial day-to-day conversations taking place in offices and plants across this country and in every industrial nation abroad. They are this minute raising or lowering the will to put out on countless jobs. Large stakes ride on what you say and how you say it.

We come now to the sixth quality that *makes* a leader. It is the warp and fiber which runs through the other five. It is so strategic to their effective use that a separate chapter is given over to it.

To summarize, here are the qualities that spell productivity and profits *now* for you as a leader.

1 . Be enthusiastic, constructive at every turn and follow through.
2 . Be persistent. Sticking with little things makes big things possible.
3 . Develop others—be flexible.
4 . Put yourself in the other person's place.
Deal with the whole individual.
5 . Express yourself clearly to be understood clearly.
6 . Build people and profits through the supreme idea.

These qualities, working through number six spell something even greater. The chapter ahead tells this story.

16

Build People Through
the Supreme Idea

This Idea is fourfold:

    a . Your future is in people and what you do to tap their unused capacity for ideas and performance.

    b . People are happiest when their talents are fully used and when they see open promotion roads ahead.

    c . The key to high productivity are people using their maximum abilities combined with the best technological skills.

    d . High productivity is the key to large cost savings, quality service to more and more customers at profits which generate new and improved products, new markets, new jobs, new earning power, new opportunities for you and your people.

Go with me inside a multiservice bank to see what this fourfold idea can do in the dramatic processing of checks. A quick picture of the strategic place of checks in the life of multitudes of people in every community is needed at this point. Over forty-four million checks are written each day drawn on sixty-seven million checking accounts in 14,000 banks in the United States. Without the processing of these checks around the clock every day and night in the year, our economy could grind to a halt.

Clark Maples, this bank's operating head, opens up an intriguing story. "Man has never created anything that is dumber than a computer. A computer cannot do anything except what you tell it to do. But our people writing programs and instructions that a computer can understand, have accomplished these kind of results in our check operations:

cost savings	— Reduced the number of those employed in the proof and bookkeeping departments by 500 at a saving of three million dollars a year.
new profitable customer services *new jobs created*	— These 500 people are in better-paying, more challenging jobs in other departments where the volume of profitable customer services increases at a rapid rate.
cost savings *fast money collections* *vital customer service*	— Multiplied the speed by which checks received from coast to coast are collected. One day's delay in collecting one million dollars in checks costs the bank $170 in interest. With four billion dollars a day in checks being processed, the money saved by fast collections carries high stakes. But the best part is a tremendous increase in service to customers.
increase in customer service *saving costs* *new jobs created* *new services to customers*	— Eliminated embarrassing mistakes in charging or crediting amounts of money to the wrong customers. The computer takes checks at the rate of 1,600 a minute, makes sure it is the right check, right amount, entered on the right customer's account, while gobbling up a five percent a year increase in volume, using 250 *less* people who moved ahead to performing varied customer services at more rewarding and satisfying work. Their new jobs include handling the entire bookkeeping operation through computers for sixty customer banks and the making up of payrolls for 100 corporations.''

Handling Mounting Blizzard of Checks

There has been much talk about a checkless society when all business will be handled electronically through debits and credits. But today even a *less* check society appears years away. So managers and supervisors in bank after bank dramatically boost productivity to meet a mounting check volume which threatens to grow from eight trillion dollars yearly in the U.S. banking system to twice that amount by the end of this decade.

Profit Sharing a Plus Result

On top of promotions and new earning power for the managers, supervisors and the individuals on the job through these large productivity gains in check handling, is each person's growing participation in the bank's profit-sharing plan.

How You Can Profit Where You Are

Harness the twin engines of productivity these managers use in processing bank checks—people and technology—to your business, your department.

Make these moves:

1. Equip your people fully with the know-why and know-how of their jobs (chapter 4, pages 51-62).
2. Link these talents to the best use of the machines and technical skills you already have while you look for even better technology in your field.

But don't stop here!

Build on These Four Principles

- Manage by objectives
- Keep within planned budgets
- Measure work
- Enlarge each manager's job

See these tools at work in the hands of Jim Blade, operating head of the rapidly growing American Service Corporation. "There is no comparison," says Blade, "between our managers of five years ago and today's producers. What has made the difference? Introducing and applying daily the four principles just cited. Through these programs our managers have tripled their performance."

Every month each one reports on the progress he is making toward previously stated goals he himself has set. His report deals with:

Volume projection. He explains the reason for any difference that occurred from the projected figure.

Manpower. He anticipated how many people he needed to handle his volume. How many does he have now in relation to volume produced? Is he using right number of people? What corrections is he making?

Pay Budget. He anticipated that in the current year it will cost him so much in salaries. If the number of people has increased to handle his volume, why? What is he doing to correct the situation? If he is five percent over or under in his projection, explain.

Space. Is he containing himself in his space? Is he utilizing it properly?

Equipment Budget. Is the equipment budgeted handling current volume? If not, what is being done?

Other Budgeting Expenses. This is the indirect cost over which he has little control. Are expenses in line? Moves he recommends if over budget.

Using management by objectives, planned budgeting, work measurement, and job enlargement, Blade expects much more out of managers and supervisors than he has ever asked before. And he is getting it. But they, too, are seeing their own goals being realized and their results rewarded in promotions and pay progress.

In work measurement, if Blade finds any of his sections producing at a seventy or eighty percent efficiency rate, he expects to receive reasons why this is happening, and what is being done to increase the output on the basis of a 100 percent (normal) standard of performance for each person on his job.

Build People by Enlarging Their Jobs

This fourth principle builds managers fast as producers. To develop people to perform at their best, be sure you write off no one—man or woman.

"Nothing in this world taught me as much about people and their untapped capacity as World War II," said Dick Laren, operating vice president of a leading merchandiser with worldwide outlets. "When our promising young talent went to war in droves, we were left with people over draft age. 'They can never pick up the ball and run with it,' we thought. But we were dead wrong. We threw them into the breach. There was no one else. We equipped them with the know-why and know-how of their new manager assignments, watched them become our best performers."

They blossomed with responsibility, asked for more, moved into management positions with relish and new energy. One of them who was thought to be "through," ("He's reached his ceiling") is today a highly respected key officer of the company.

Never discount anyone. Right now individuals in company after company, possessing uncovered talents, would have died on the vine if a superior, alert to mining these talents, had not given them their chance. Such persons could well be in your department, your company. People are rising to grab their opportunities in every field, but it often must be triggered by a boss who has this leadership quality.

Arthur Randley, a janitor for years in a company which is a leader in the financial field, was given the chance to become a computer programmer because his manager *believed he could do it*. On his own initiative he had completed electrical data processing courses at night. Today he heads his organization's computer programming department, and is considered one of the finest experts in the business.

Fred West was pigeonholed, forever it seemed to him, in one section of the Del Ray Company, analyzing profit-sharing plans for corporate customers. But his manager who made a practice of *knowing* the abilities of each person reporting to him saw an opportunity to recommend Fred for something much bigger. Now he directs the benefit and incentive plans for his entire company, including profit sharing, pension, insurance, hospitalization and the rapidly growing suggestion system. A whole new world has suddenly opened up with a chance to use his imagination and ideas in many directions. "My big motivation," West points out, "comes from the satisfaction I get out of a job like this."

Dan North, of Martin's Consolidated, supervisor in the same type of operations for ten years, has recently been made responsible for four production divisions instead of one. "I've had a barrel-full of problems put in my lap and I love it," he said. "There is no one who enjoys his job more than I do." His pay, now doubled, gives that enjoyment new dimensions. Best of all, he sees a promotion road ahead he never before thought possible.

Arthur Randley, Fred West, Dan North. Their stories could be multiplied many times in today's U.S. work force of more than eighty million individual men and women. Here is people power linked with idea power. There has never been any power like it up to now. Yet it is still virtually untapped. We have only begun to mine this giant reservoir of productive talents at a time that could prove to be the turning point for man's upward thrust to a new era of progress for every person.

". . . It Could Blow Up Mankind!"

Inside the squash courts, under the stands of the University of Chicago's Stagg Field, on December 2, 1942, our friend and eminent physicist, Dr. Robert Moon, with his secret group, gazed awe-stricken at what they had wrought—the first self-sustaining nuclear chain reaction. It was the birth of the Atomic Age.

These nuclear scientists, initially financed by a kitty of $33,000 from President Roosevelt, starting out in 1936 to show that an atom bomb couldn't be made, had found that it could be. They shook with the realization of what their discovery meant—the moral inplication of living in a nuclear era. "We were absolutely stunned by the knowledge of the power we had in our hands," said Dr. Moon, "and the question was, 'Can we afford to let this secret out?' It could blow up mankind!"

From 1942 to July 16, 1945, the first testing of the atomic bomb, the group's lips were sealed. Not even their wives knew. During this period they petitioned the President to introduce the bomb on some uninhabited island. Let all the world have the secret.

Seventeen days before it happened, President Truman asked them whether they would recommend dropping the bomb on Hiroshima, Japan. The Group voted "no" but confronted with the awful pressure to end the war and stop the killing of American boys, its chairman, Dr. Arthur Compton, finally answered "yes."

After Hiroshima the scientists cried. The drive for their whole project had been a discovery for helping instead of destroying. As Dr. Moon put it, "All through this assignment we felt God was working through us for human progress.'' Later, on the group's strong recommendation, the secret of nuclear energy was released to the Free World.

Now we have the hydrogen bomb, not a military weapon, which kills tens of millions of people at one stroke without discrimination.

Power Unlimited to Build

Today each manager, supervisor and president holds in his hands a totally different kind of power, and far more potent, the power to build, never to destroy—the power to develop the vast untapped resources of the individual person to meet vital, fast-changing needs. You draw on this power each time you take hold of and apply the Five Keys to Productivity and Profits for constructive goals in human progress.

When you help each individual unlock his talents to the full, linking them to his use of the *best* technological skills continually being discovered, you give him control over his own future, open up for him and for you dynamic careers of service which bring the kind of rewards you get in no other way.